#Hou

What if there had been social media during the Apollo 13 Moon mission?

This is not a book in the usual book format. It is the story of the incredible Apollo 13 mission in 1970 told as if in real time in the form of imaginary social media posts written by the main participants and observers. The narrative is based on astronaut accounts, NASA transcripts of the astronauts' conversations with Mission Control and live broadcasts of the major U.S. TV networks covering the unfolding drama hour by hour.

There is a list of major sources at the back of the book.

Apollo 13 was a mission that gripped the entire nation and the world. It would test the courage, endurance and ingenuity, not just of three astronauts but also of the thousands of controllers, technicians and engineers back at Mission Control in Houston and across America.

Thursday 9 April, 1970

Two days before launch

Jim Lovell

James Arthur Lovell Jr. was the commander of the Apollo 13 mission in April, 1970; the mission intended to be the third NASA mission to land astronauts on the surface of the Moon. Prior to the Apollo 13 mission, Lovell had flown on the Gemini 7 and Gemini 12 missions, and had been the command module pilot of the Apollo 8 mission - the first Apollo mission to put a manned spacecraft in orbit around the Moon.

Jim Lovell @JLCDRApollo13
After two years of meticulous preparation and training, we are now just two days away from setting off for the Moon.

Jim Lovell @JLCDRApollo13
I for one could not feel more ready for this. I'm sure Fred Haise and Ken Mattingly feel just the same.

Walter Cronkite @WCronkiteCBSNews
Apollo 13: a new and dangerous voyage to one of the oldest areas of the Moon and the riskiest lunar landing yet attempted, lies ahead for Jim Lovell, Fred Haise and Ken Mattingly.

Walter Cronkite @WCronkiteCBSNews
Just 2 days to go now before the launch of this the third mission to land men on the surface of the Moon. Unlike its two predecessors, Apollo 13 is going into very rugged, lunar highland areas.

Walter Cronkite @WCronkiteCBSNews
The lunar module Aquarius will stay on the Moon for 33 hours, during which time astronauts Jim Lovell and Fred Haise will take two long moonwalks.

Jules Bergman @JBABCNews
Apollo 13 will attempt to land in Frau Mauro, a rough, hilly highland area similar to the foothills of the Rockies.

Jules Bergman @JBABCNews
The area is littered with debris from a mammoth meteorite impact, offering chunks of the Moon 5 billion years old.

Wally Schirra @WSchirraNASA
Lovell and Haise will conduct scientific experiments, set up a scientific base station, and hopefully send back the first color television pictures from the Moon's surface.

Wally Schirra @WSchirraNASA
Ken Mattingly will be circling overhead in the command ship.

Jules Bergman @JBABCNews
To solve the mystery of whether the Moon is dead or has a hot core like the Earth, Haise will drill three 10-feet deep holes with a battery-powered electric drill.

Jules Bergman @JBABCNews
Haise will then slip a series of heat measuring devices in two of the holes to detect the precise temperature differences beneath the surface.

Jules Bergman @JBABCNews
The third hole will be used to collect a sample of Moon's crust from 9 or 10 feet below the surface.

Jules Bergman @JBABCNews
On the second moonwalk, they'll hike two miles to a high-rimmed crater to get pictures and samples to see how it got there and what has happened to it.

Walter Cronkite @WCronkiteCBSNews
If it all seems routine, if it seems to lack the wild suspense and drama of Apollo 11, perhaps there's a lesson for all of us in men who are willing to press on, facing new dangers for new learning, even if they weren't there first.

Jim Lovell @JLCDRApollo13
On my way now to see Deke Slayton, Director of Flight Crew operations. Something of great urgency seems to have come up.

Walter Cronkite (1916-2009)

Walter Cronkite was best known as the main anchorman for the American CBS television news network during much of the Cold War in the 1950s, 1960s and 1970s. Often referred to as "the most trusted man in America", Cronkite was the face of American news during the Cuban Missile Crisis, the assassinations of Martin Luther King, John F. Kennedy and Robert Kennedy; throughout the American space program, Moon landings and the war in Vietnam.

Walter Cronkite @WCronkiteCBSNews
With just hours to go before lift off of Apollo 13, there is the possibility tonight that a case of German measles could delay the flight of Apollo 13.

Walter Cronkite @WCronkiteCBSNews
NASA says that one of the backup crew, Charlie Duke, was exposed to a child with the disease at the weekend.

Walter Cronkite @WCronkiteCBSNews
Two of the three members of the prime crew, Lovell and Haise, have been found to have immunity to the disease. The third, command module pilot Ken Mattingly, does not.

Deke Slayton @DSDrctrFlghtCrwOps
I had some very bad news to deliver to the Apollo 13 crew. Charlie Duke has the measles and all the crew have been exposed to it. We believe Ken Mattingly may have caught the disease.

Wally Schirra @WSchirraNASA
The NASA doctors fear that with the measles incubation period, Ken Mattingly would develop the disease during the time he is alone and in control of the command module.

Wally Schirra @WSchirraNASA
There is therefore the possibility of a delay, or of replacing Mattingly with one of the backup crew members.

Walter Cronkite @WCronkiteCBSNews
The disease only lasts for a few days, but for Mattingly those would be the wrong few days. If they have to postpone the flight until the next possible launch date, it would cost close to a million dollars.

Walter Cronkite @WCronkiteCBSNews
The only way doctors could guarantee that Mattingly will not get sick during the mission would be if he got sick before and recovered.

Walter Cronkite @WCronkiteCBSNews
For the past 2 days, everyone has been watching Mattingly closely hoping he would get sick, but so far he's refused to cooperate.

Wally Schirra @WSchirraNASA
A postponement of the flight would amount to a million-dollar case of measles—the most expensive case of measles in the history of the world.

Wally Schirra @WSchirraNASA
One of the backup crew, Jack Swiggert, is being given extra simulator time to increase his readiness should he replace Mattingly, but there is considerable resistance to breaking up the crew.

Wally Schirra @WSchirraNASA
This is a crew that has trained together for two years. A final decision has to be made by Friday night.

Walter Cronkite @WCronkiteCBSNews
Meanwhile, the countdown goes on and the weather outlook now is good. Ken Mattingly has been briefing Jack Swigert (a 38-year-old civilian bachelor space rookie) on the flight plans.

Walter Cronkite @WCronkiteCBSNews
Swigert's job would be to fly the command module while Lovell and Haise are on the Moon.

Jules Bergman @JBABCNews
If NASA go ahead and replace Mattingly with Swigert, he will have only 48 hours to try to develop the kind of teamwork with the other crew members that normally takes months—quite an assignment.

Wally Schirra @WSchirraNASA
As mission commander Jim Lovell's personal feelings are likely to be that the flight should be delayed a month to allow Mattingly to fly. But he is well aware of the huge costs and logistics that would be involved in such a delay.

Wally Schirra @WSchirraNASA
A lot of people are brought on at the last minute to do the multitude of pre-launch tasks. A lot of people are brought down from Houston and all over the country.

Wally Schirra @WSchirraNASA
Tracking station teams are deployed all over the world now for this and they're all in place now and prepared to get to work.

Jules Bergman @JBABCNews
Whether the flight goes on Saturday hinges on Jack Swigert's ability to be ready in time. It's almost a soap opera script with a life and death plot.

Jules Bergman @JBABCNews
Can a backup pilot, who hasn't had all the final training, fly on the most complex lunar mission we've yet attempted and do everything just right?

Jules Bergman @JBABCNews
Well-informed sources within NASA say that Jim Lovell, the Apollo13 commander, is urging NASA management to wait and scrub the flight for a month so Mattingly can get over the measles he may get and fly.

Walter Cronkite @WCronkiteCBSNews
Chief astronaut Deke Slayton who came up with the idea of putting Swigert in is the man in the fire. He's the man responsible for isolating crews before a flight.

Walter Cronkite @WCronkiteCBSNews
Had the astronauts been isolated for 21 days as the medics wanted, the measles threat would never have developed.

Deke Slayton (1925–1993)

Donald Kent Slayton had been a U.S. Army Air Force B-25 bomber pilot during World War II, flying missions over both Europe and Japan. Following the war, he gained a BSc in aeronautical engineering and became a test pilot for the Air Force's supersonic fighter aircraft. In 1959, he was chosen as one of the Mercury Program's original seven astronauts but was later grounded due to a minor heart condition and did not fly in the program. He later became NASA's director of flight crew operations and was responsible for deciding the makeup of Apollo crews, including who would be the first astronaut to set foot on the Moon.

Deke Slayton @DSDrctrFlghtCrwOps
We will have to take Ken off the mission. Jim hates the decision but we can't take the risk.

Jules Bergman @JBABCNews
Today, Dr. Tom Payne, the Space Agency chief told us NASA will institute new isolation rules in future.

Jules Bergman @JBABCNews
Payne will make the final decision on the launch tomorrow after talking with mission commander Lovell and other officials. It's 50-50.

Jim Lovell @JLCDRApollo13
I can't accept breaking up my crew at this point. After all these months of training together we are perfectly attuned to each other's thoughts, movements and actions.

Deke Slayton @DSDrctrFlghtCrwOps
Jack Swigert will be a perfectly fine replacement as command module pilot. He's been through the identical training as Mattingly.

Jim Lovell @JLCDRApollo13
Deke is wrong. Swigert is an excellent pilot but he hasn't been in the flight simulator for weeks.

Deke Slayton @DSDrctrFlghtCrwOps
Jim will just have to bite the bullet. He can either accept Swigert as Mattingly's replacement as command module pilot or be bumped, along with his crew, to a later mission.

Jim Lovell @JLCDRApollo13
I think these crew changes are wrong, but what can I do? It's either lose Ken Mattingly or lose the Moon... I'm not going to lose the Moon.

Ken Mattingly @KMLMPilotApollo13
I don't have the measles. I'm not gonna get the measles. This just isn't right. Those medical guys are being cautious to a ridiculous degree.

Deke Slayton @DKDrctrFlghtCrwOps
Even if Ken has only a one in a thousand chance of getting sick, it's a risk we can't take. As pilot of the command module, he has to be 110% fit, 110% of the time.

Jim Lovell @JLCDRApollo13
I feel so bad for Ken. We all do. I even feel bad for Deke—he's the one who has to take heartbreaking decisions like this. Ken will still have his chance on later missions.

Deke Slayton @DKDrctrFlghtCrwOps
I've got broad shoulders. I'll be in Ken's corner further down the line, but right now we have to do everything possible to ensure the success of Apollo 13. Jack Swigert will be a fine command module pilot.

Thomas Payne @TPayneDirNASA
The evidence is substantial that about the time we would have been conducting the lunar operation, Mattingly would be coming down with symptoms of the measles and his capacity for carrying out command module operations would be questionable.

Thomas Payne (1921-1992)

Thomas Payne was an American scientist, administrator and manager. He had been tasked with getting the Apollo program back on track after the Apollo 1 disaster and was the most senior NASA administrator during the Apollo 11 Moon landing and several other Apollo missions including Apollo 13. He was also involved in preparing plans for the post-Apollo era, including plans for establishing a lunar base and a manned mission to Mars by 1981. However, those plans were never taken up by the political leadership in Washington.

Thomas Payne @TPayneDirNASA
I met with Jim Lovell and Fred Haise again in a private meeting. We discussed all the aspects of the mission and their feelings about it.

Thomas Payne @TPayneDirNASA
In all the recent meetings we have had, the unanimous decision is that the Apollo 13 mission be launched tomorrow.

Walter Cronkite @WCronkiteCBSNews
And so it has been decided. Jack Swigert will replace Ken Mattingly as command module pilot and the mission will go ahead in accordance with the pre-existing schedule.

Walter Cronkite @WCronkiteCBSNews
The decision came after Swigert had gone through a battery of last-minute tests to determine how well he could team up with the other two crewmen. That decision involved a good deal of agonizing.

Thomas Payne @TPayneDirNASA
We understand that Ken Mattingly is disappointed and depressed at being dropped from the mission, but they say he is taking it philosophically and there's every chance that he will be included in future Moon missions.

Jules Bergman @JBABCNews
The final decision may have been unanimous, but there is no question about the attitude of the spacecraft commander, James Lovell.

Jules Bergman @JBABCNews
Lovell argued today that Mattingly, even with German measles, would still have been preferable as command module pilot.

Jules Bergman @JBABCNews
Lovell's argument was made without prejudice to the new man Jack Swigert. For the past two days, Swigert has been intensively practicing spaceship operations where three men must work as one.

Thomas Payne @TPayneDirNASA
Swigert has performed well against an extremely tough deadline, but nobody pretends that he has had as much practice as the man he replaces.

Gene Kranz @GKFlgtDirApollo13
To make things easier for Swigert, we have dropped some of the complex photographic tasks assigned to the command module pilot.

Jules Bergman @JBABCNews
The decision to go ahead with the mission seems to represent NASA management more than it does the astronauts themselves.

Jules Bergman @JBABCNews
There is no question that the pressures on Jim Lovell and Fred Haise have increased greatly. Not to mention the pressure on the new man—Jack Swigert.

Jack Swigert (1931-1982)

Jack Swigert was a former test pilot and before joining NASA had obtained a BSc in Mechanical Engineering and a Masters degree in Aerospace Engineering. He joined NASA's Astronaut Group Five in 1966, becoming a specialist on the Apollo command module. He was the only unmarried astronaut among the early NASA astronauts. Just two days before the scheduled launch of Apollo 13, Swigert was brought in to replace command module pilot Ken Mattingly who NASA doctors believed had been exposed to the measles virus.

Jack Swigert @JSCMPApollo13
Sitting in the simulator with Jim and Freddo. About to practice Earth re-entry procedures.

Jim Lovell @JLCDRApollo13
The simulator technicians are throwing Jack curveballs, having us coming in too shallow and then too deep. Actual re-entry is not going to be like that.

Jack Swigert @JSCMPApollo13
Oh, man! That was one hell of a simulation. One day before launch and I've just piloted the command module simulator through Earth re-entry and fried all three of us.

Jim Lovell @JLCDRApollo13
That wasn't the first time we've died in the simulator. Hope Jack isn't feeling too bad about it. Neil Armstrong crashed the lunar module into the Moon many times in the simulator—didn't hurt them in the real deal.

Deke Slayton @DKDrctrFlghtCrwOps
I've told the simulator technicians to run the re-entry simulation again. Jack needs as much practice as we can cram in during these final hours before launch.

Walter Cronkite @WCronkiteCBSNews
We're looking down at Apollo 13 from the top of the launch tower and as of now that big bird is all set for take off for the Moon on schedule at 2.13 p.m. Eastern Time tomorrow.

Saturday
11 April, 1970

Launch Day

Fred Haise

After working with NASA as a civilian research pilot, Fred Wallace Haise Jr. was selected as one of 19 new NASA astronauts selected for Astronaut Group 5 in 1966. Before joining the crew of Apollo 13, Haise had been the backup lunar module pilot for the Apollo 8 and Apollo 11 missions. As pilot of the lunar module, Haise would have become only the sixth man to walk on the surface of the Moon.

Fred Haise @FHLMPilotApollo13
Sitting alongside Jim and Jack atop the giant Saturn V rocket. No more simulations now. This is the real deal. Feels different too—I don't recall this much thumping in my chest during any of the simulations.

Jim Lovell @JLCDRApollo13
Flight Director is about to run through the 'GO-NO GO' checklist now. Hoping for a perfect series of GOs. I don't want to have to climb out and back to ground level again.

Walter Cronkite @WCronkiteCBSNews
Under reasonably-clear skies, a high haze still but no serious weather problems, we're waiting for the launch of Apollo 13 with just some 21 minutes and 20 seconds left in the countdown before the launch.

Walter Cronkite @WCronkiteCBSNews
Apollo 13 is about to set off on a half a million mile voyage, four days around the Moon and back to Earth likely right on time and within a couple of miles of the planned landing zone in the Pacific—which is quite remarkable when you think about it.

Walter Cronkite @WCronkiteCBSNews
We had some reference to the number 13 earlier. Of course, the number 13 is considered by some to be an unlucky number.

Walter Cronkite @WCronkiteCBSNews
It is Apollo flight number 13, it is taking off at 2.13, they'll be the 13th., 14th. and 15th. men to go to the Moon, but nobody seems at all concerned at all about the numerology involved.

Chuck Hollinshead @CHLaunchControl
Countdown is moving well at this time. T minus 19 minutes 4 seconds and counting.

Walter Cronkite @WCronkiteCBSNews
The U.S. Vice President and the West German Chancellor are among the many thousands of special guests invited to watch the launch today.

Walter Cronkite @WCronkiteCBSNews
The German Chancellor has reason to be proud—many of the important people in our space program came from the German rocket program.

Walter Cronkite @WCronkiteCBSNews
Those German rocket engineers came to U.S. immediately after World War II of their own volition we are told, choosing the U.S. over Russia.

Walter Cronkite @WCronkiteCBSNews
I've just learned that one of the Lovell's children has measles. I saw Jim Lovell's wife Marilyn last night. Unlike Lovell, I've not had measles, so I have no immunity.

Walter Cronkite @WCronkiteCBSNews
I'm assuming therefore that CBS is going to remove me from the rest of this broadcast and turn it over to my colleague Wally Schirra here.

Walter Cronkite @WCronkiteCBSNews
Just joking there. Wally and I will be together throughout this epic voyage of scientific exploration.

Gene Kranz @GKFlgtDirApollo13
Wearing my latest special lucky vest for the mission much to the sarcastic delight of everyone here at

Mission Control. About to run through the checklist for the last time.

Gene Kranz

Gene Kranz was the lead flight director during the Apollo 13 Moon mission. He and his team (the White Team) were on duty at Mission Control in Houston when the explosion in the service module occurred and were responsible for instituting the critical consumption constraints of electricity, oxygen and water during those crucial first few moments and hours as well as the course correction burns and power-up procedures. Kranz and his team later received the Presidential Medal of Freedom from President Nixon for their efforts.

Gene Kranz @GKFlgtDirApollo13
Booster, Retro, FIDO, Guidance, Surgeon and EECOM are all 'GO'.

Gene Kranz @GKFlgtDirApollo13
GNC, Telemetry, Control, Procedures, INCO, FAO and Network all report a 'GO'.

Deke Slayton @DKDrctrFlghtCrwOps
Looking good.

Chuck Hollinshead @CHLaunchControl
We're keeping an eye on that power transfer at T minus 1 minute and 50 seconds.

Chuck Hollinshead @CHLaunchControl
The propellant is now all pressurized. That's the third stage of the Saturn rocket. One minute 15 seconds and counting.

Chuck Hollinshead @CHLaunchControl
We're now approaching the T minus one minute mark.

Chuck Hollinshead @CHLaunchControl
T minus one minute and counting. Power transfer is taking place: first stage... second stage... third stage.

Gene Kranz @GKFlgtDirApollo13
The instrument unit is going to internal power. T minus 45 seconds and the count continues to go well.

Gene Kranz @GKFlgtDirApollo13
We are looking for an ignition of those 5 first stage engines at the T minus 8 point 9 seconds mark.

Chuck Hollinshead @CHLaunchControl
T minus 35 seconds and counting.

Gene Kranz @GKFlgtDirApollo13
Recovery and CAPCOM are both GO! Handing over to Launch Control at Cape Kennedy.

Chuck Hollinshead @CHLaunchControl
We are 'GO' for launch.

Chuck Hollinshead @CHLaunchControl
20 seconds....

Chuck Hollinshead @CHLaunchControl
12, 11, 10, 9...

Chuck Hollinshead @CHLaunchControl
7, 6...ignition sequence starts...

Chuck Hollinshead @CHLaunchControl
3, 2, 1... and lift off of Apollo 13... en route to the Moon.

Jim Lovell @JLCDRApollo13
The clock is running.

Jack Swigert @JSCMPApollo13
We have cleared the tower.

Jim Lovell @JLCDRApollo13
Roll complete and we are pitching.

Joe Kerwin @JKerwinCAPCOM
Apollo 13 is 'GO' at 30 seconds.

Jack Swigert @JSCMPApollo13
Altitude correct. Velocity optimal.

Joe Kerwin @JKerwinCAPCOM
At one minute seven seconds, we show an altitude of 4.1 nautical miles, downrange 1 mile. We are GO for staging.

Joe Kerwin @JKerwinCAPCOM
Apollo 13 first stage separation confirmed.

Jim Lovell @JLCDRApollo13
I have initiated guidance at 3 minutes 33 seconds.

Joe Kerwin @JKerwinCAPCOM
Trajectory is good. Thrust is good.

Joe Kerwin @JKerwinCAPCOM
Apollo 13 remains 'GO' at 4 minutes. Coming up to 5 minutes. Looking perfect.

Fred Haise @FHLMPilotApollo13
We just felt a huge jolt... before the first stage separated, not after separation as is supposed to happen.

Jim Lovell @JLCDRApollo13
Center engine has just cut out!

Joe Kerwin @JKerwinCAPCOM
We have confirmed inboard engine has cut out. That is not supposed to happen yet.

Gene Kranz @GKFlgtDirApollo13
One engine cut out is not critical, we can burn the remaining engines a little longer. But if another one goes we will have to abort.

Joe Kerwin @JKerwinCAPCOM
Apollo 13 remains 'GO' at 6 minutes 13 seconds. We don't have the story on why inboard engine 5 cut out early, but Apollo 13 remains 'GO' at this time.

Jim Lovell @JLCDRApollo13
Every flight has to have its own glitch. Hopefully, we just had ours and it'll be plain sailing from here on in.

Joe Kerwin @JKerwinCAPCOM
Apollo 13 is looking good at 8 minutes 10 seconds.

Wally Schirra @WSchirraNASA
Apollo 13 is standing by for next staging.

Fred Haise @FHLMPilotApollo13
Sustainer engine cut off. Second staging completed.

Jim Lovell @JLCDRApollo13
Twelve minutes and 34 seconds and we are now approaching Earth orbit.

Wally Schirra @WSchirraNASA
At over 12 minutes, that was the longest burn time I can remember. They had to do the longer burn due to the early cut off of engine number 5.

Jim Lovell @JLCDRApollo13
We are now in Earth orbit.

Joe Kerwin @JKerwinCAPCOM
Apollo 13's preliminary orbit looks good from down here. We're working on why number 5 engine cut out early - we don't need to go through that again!

Jim Lovell @JLCDRApollo13
There's nothing like an interesting launch, and we're just coming up on a beautiful sunrise.

Jack Swigert @JSCMPApollo13
Uh oh! Freddo's just started throwing up.

Fred Haise @FHLMPilotApollo13
I'm okay. Just that my large breakfast didn't take too kindly to that huge jolt we got at first stage separation.

Gene Kranz @GKFlgtDirApollo13
The flight surgeons report Freddo's biodata telemetry shows no problem. He's about to start filming from inside the capsule with one of the onboard cameras.

Fred Haise @FHLMPilotApollo13
Nothing to film outside right now - too much cloud cover. I'll send them some footage of Jim just so they'll know he's still here.

Jack Swigert @JSCMPApollo13
We're coming up over some land now. Hope the folks back home get to this on their TVs when Freddo starts filming. Looks like we've just crossed over the Gulf of Mexico.

Joe Kerwin @JKerwinCAPCOM
Apollo 13 has a GO on all systems. Oxygen flow check remains nominal at this time. No sweat.

Jack Swigert @JSCMPApollo13
On course now to detach from the booster, turn the command module around and dock with the lunar module which is docked in the nose of the Saturn booster.

Jack Swigert @JSCMPApollo13
We have successfully separated from the Saturn booster and are now maneuvering.

Fred Haise @FHLMPilotApollo13
Jack is lining up with my lunar module Aquarius now. Hoping for a clean capture.

Jack Swigert @JSCMPApollo13
Thrusting forward... slowly...100 feet to docking.

Fred Haise @FHLMPilotApollo13
40 feet... 30... 20... 10 feet.

Jack Swigert @JSCMPApollo13
Captured! Confirmed to Houston that we have a hard dock with the lunar module.

Jack Swigert @JSCMPApollo13
We are now pulling Aquarius away from its Saturn IV rocket housing.

DOCKING AND SEPARATION OF SPACECRAFT FROM S IV B

Illustration: The command and service module (Odyssey) docking with the lunar module (Aquarius) housed in the Saturn booster.

Deke Slayton @DKDrctrFlghtCrwOps
Jack did a real tidy job of capturing the lunar module. That confirms that insisting he replace Mattingly was the right decision. Something of a relief for me personally.

Jim Lovell @JLCDRApollo13
We have completed systems attachments between the command and lunar modules.

Fred Haise @FHLMPilotApollo13
Now about to start the TV broadcast for the folks back on Earth.

4 hours mission time

Joe Kerwin @JKerwinCAPCOM
Apollo 13 is cleared for fuel cell purge and water dump at their discretion. I'm handing over to Vance Brand who will be CAPCOM for the next shift.

Fred Haise @FHLMPilotApollo13
There's a slight burn smell up in the tunnel area between Odyssey and Aquarius.

Wally Schirra @WSchirraNASA
The burn smell in the tunnel area has been reported on previous flights. It's never amounted to a problem.

Jim Lovell @JLCDRApollo13
We are about to do a fuel cell purge and waste water dump.

Fred Haise @FHLMPilotApollo13
We are venting urine into space on schedule. I can see thousands of particles passing by outside... Beautiful!

Jack Swigert @JSCMPApollo13
We are powering up the lunar module now.

Vance Brand @VBrandCAPCOM
The crew are getting some great-looking pictures of Earth out of the window right now. We need to record those camera f-settings for future photography.

Jack Swigert @JSCMPApollo13
When we went back up the tunnel, we found two latches that weren't cocked. We reset them.

Jack Swigert @JSCMPApollo13
Wow! That is such a beautiful view of Earth out of window one.

Fred Haise @FHLMPilotApollo13
The windows came through launch in good shape Window 3 looks real clean. Looks like that Hycon stuff is pretty good.

Fred Haise @FHLMPilotApollo13
Seeing what look like two contrails out of the window now. One above and one below. It's a very pretty sight.

Ken Mattingly @KMLMPilotApollo13
I followed the launch all the way up. Didn't see the staging – it was too hazy for that, but I could see it for a few miles. Looked like a really interesting ride.

Jim Lovell @JLCDRApollo13
We're going to take some specialized Earth weather photography. I have the camera directed down at Earth and am about to start shooting.

Jim Lovell @JLCDRApollo13
We have spent the last hour or so mainly concerned with Earth photography, and I believe we have captured some images for the ages.

Vance Brand @VBrandCAPCOM
We can let Apollo 13 know about every two minutes before Earth should be coming into view in their window. We think we've got it pegged down pretty well now.

Fred Haise @FHLMPilotApollo13
I guess the world really does turn. I can see some landmasses now. It must be Australia down near the bottom, and over to the left... some part of Asia... China probably.

Vance Brand @VBrandCAPCOM
Now that astronaut Fred Haise has verified from actual observation that Earth does in fact turn, I guess we can call this Haise's theory, huh?

Jack Swigert @JSCMPApollo13
Altitude computations now show us as 55,000 miles out. No longer in orbit but en route to the Moon.

Vance Brand @VBrandCAPCOM
Swigert just told us that they have a sign under their LEB DSKY saying, "My name is Hal." I told him to be nice to Hal. He assured me they would be.

Jim Lovell @JLCDRApollo13
I have told Houston that we have taken 10 Earth photography window pictures and are now ready to bed down for the night. They asked for just one more picture and then it's goodnight all.

View of the receding Earth as seen from Apollo 13

Fred Haise @FHLMPilotApollo13
Nice music – Halls of Montezuma. Good stuff to have on a long voyage.

Vance Brand @VBrandCAPCOM
We're registering MASTER ALARMS. Freddo says it's another oxygen high level that he is monitoring and testing. No problem.

Vance Brand @VBrandCAPCOM
We think the spacecraft is in pretty good shape. Nobody down here has any comment as to why our astronauts should not hit the hay right now after a pretty good day's work.

Jim Lovell @JLCDRApollo13
Goodnight Houston – it has been a long day. Goodnight Earth people.

23 hours mission time

Joe Kerwin @JKerwinCAPCOM
The Apollo 13 crew should be awake and alert right now having had what seems like an uneventful night's sleep.

Jim Lovell @JLCDRApollo13
We all slept pretty well on board Apollo 13 last night after a long and action-packed day's work yesterday.

Joe Kerwin @JKerwinCAPCOM
We are getting a report ready for Apollo 13 regarding their onboard consumables. Other than that, the only thing to report on the spacecraft is that it is getting farther away from Earth.

Jim Lovell @JLCDRApollo13
The flight surgeon asked us to each give a rough estimate of the number of hours we slept and a qualitative assessment, i.e. good, fair or poor. We all indicated 5 to 6 hours, quality 'good'.

Joe Kerwin @JKerwinCAPCOM
We need to verify that the crew cycled the oxygen cryo fans. We saw the hydrogen fans cycled but didn't see the oxygen tanks get stirred up.

Joe Kerwin @JKerwinCAPCOM
The cryos are as follows: Hydrogen tank 1: 83%. Hydrogen tank 2: 86%. Oxygen tank 1: 87%. Oxygen tank 2: 87%

Jim Lovell @JLCDRApollo13
All the levels on the cryo tanks are better than optimal at this stage in the mission. We're in good shape.

Jim Lovell @JLCDRApollo13
Joe just updated us with the latest news from Planet Earth: The Astros survived 8 to 7. The Cubs were rained out. There were earthquakes in Manila and other areas of Luzon Island.

Jim Lovell @JLCDRApollo13
The Beatles have announced that they will break up. They are reported to have earned more than a half billion dollars in their career. However, rumors that they will use this money to start their own space program are said to be false.

Jack Swigert @JSCMPApollo13
Houston also reminded us that income taxes need to be filed in the coming days. Damn! I will need an extension on mine.

Joe Kerwin @JKerwinCAPCOM
Swigert just asked if we could arrange an extension on his tax return and Lovell asked if it was true Swigert's tax return was going to be used to buy fuel for the lunar module. Good stuff!

Joe Kerwin @JKerwinCAPCOM
Jim McDivit asked me to tell Fred Haise that he forgot to fuel the ascent stage of the lunar module. Much hilarity here at Mission Control at the moment.

Joe Kerwin @JKerwinCAPCOM
We've had a weather update for the splashdown area in the mid-Pacific. There is a small weather avoidance issue – there is a weather area 20 degrees south of the landing area, but it is moving south.

Jim Lovell @JLCDRApollo13
I have completed the noise and vibration evaluations we made of the launch and separation stages and relayed it to Mission Control. Nothing of major concern to report.

Jim Lovell @JLCDRApollo13
Comparing this flight to Apollo 8, there was about the same level of vibration, but there were a couple more big jolts during second stage separation.

Jim Lovell @JLCDRApollo13
I just made myself a hotdog sandwich with catsup. Very tasty and almost unheard of in the old days. We

have about four different methods of spreading catsup in zero gravity now.

30 hours mission time

Jack Swigert @JSCMPApollo13
Houston just informed me that I may get a 60 day extension on filing my income tax if I am out of the country... I guess I qualify right now.

Jack Swigert @JSCMPApollo13
We're a bit ahead of ourselves and I asked if we have a GO to do the next fuel cell purge and waste water dump.

Jack Swigert @JSCMPApollo13
We do have a GO.

Jack Swigert @JSCMPApollo13
We also have a GO for the next TV broadcast at the scheduled time. That's great because we have a beautiful sight to show the folks back home.

Vance Brand @VBrandCAPCOM
Jim is holding the camera looking out of window 3 directly at the Moon. The Sun came out and we saw about 30 seconds of the waste water dump. It looked fantastic! Jack is complaining about seeing stars.

Jim Lovell @JLCDRApollo13
It's amazing watching those little frozen droplets maneuver. They seem to go out in all directions, but when they get out a certain ways and settle down, they all seem to be travelling in the same direction.

Jack Swigert @JSCMPApollo13
We are now at the correct attitude for the scheduled non-free return course correction burn. Jim is on the sextant and we do have a star in the sextant.

Fred Haise @FHLMPilotApollo13
We are at course correction burn time minus six minutes.

Jack Swigert @JSCMPApollo13
Burning now. 40%...60%...80%...Yaw and pitch both good.

Jack Swigert @JSCMPApollo13
Scheduled burn and associated maneuvers completed. No problem. Everything went fine. On course for the Moon with no problems and none anticipated.

Jack Swigert @JSCMPApollo13
I'm asking the computer how far away we are, and it is telling me we are now 121,490 miles out. Roughly half way to the Moon.

Vance Brand @VBrandCAPCOM
Jim says it's impossible to comb their hair in zero gravity. At least their beards haven't yet come along to the point where they will need to use a razor. That will likely be a real mess.

Jack Swigert @JSCMPApollo13
Houston just told me the Masters golf tournament was a tie after 72 holes. There will be a playoff on Monday. Sounds exciting.

Fred Haise @FHLMPilotApollo13
The camera is now showing sparkling particles going across the screen. Those are being emitted from the thrusters. Jack is maneuvering the spacecraft.

Jim Lovell @JLCDRApollo13
Showing the folks back on Earth the answer to the age-old question of how we get rid of our waste products. They can see it goes right outside when we open up the waste dump.

Vance Brand @VBrandCAPCOM
Speed of Apollo 13 with respect to the Earth is now 4,667 feet per second.

Jim Lovell @JLCDRApollo13
We are preparing our sleep stations - hammocks. They are actually quite comfortable. When we first heard about them, we thought they weren't necessary, but they turned out to be very nice devices to sleep in.

Vance Brand @VBrandCAPCOM
We would like Apollo 13 to get some pictures of Bennet's Comet which they are now in a position to do. However, the camera stability requirement is very high, so if they could sketch it, that would be great.

Jack Swigert @JSCMPApollo13
We are noticing that there is a slight distinction in the flow of hydrogen versus the flow of oxygen.

Vance Brand @VBrandCAPCOM
We see that the flow of hydrogen versus the flow of oxygen is exactly matched, so it might be a purely spacecraft read-out problem.

Jim Lovell @JLCDRApollo13
The cryo pressure light has come on. The hydrogen tank has hit its lower bound. I'm asking Houston if they want us to go back to AUTO on hydrogen heater 1.

Vance Brand @VBrandCAPCOM
I told Apollo 13 they should leave the hydrogen cryo switch in the OFF position until they go to bed. Just before they turn in, we'll turn the switch to AUTO.

Jack Swigert @JSCMPApollo13
I just had a conversation with Ken Mattingly whom I replaced as command module pilot. He was very helpful regarding the numbers behind some of the photo targets.

Vance Brand @VBrandCAPCOM
FIDO says he's concerned that the Apollo 13 crew have been doing a lot of waste water dumping. They're jiggling around again after the latest dump.

Jim Lovell @JLCDRApollo13
I have just changed another lithium hydroxide canister. I hear the Flight Dynamics Officer (FIDO) is concerned about our waste water dumping.

Vance Brand @VBrandCAPCOM
FIDO now says he's pacified after Swigert's past comments on their trajectory, and he hasn't seen any waste water dumps for a while now so he's happy. He anticipates no more mid-course corrections from this point.

Jim Lovell @JLCDRApollo13
Houston has told us that we may be able to move up our transfer to the lunar module to give us more familiarization time. If there are no more mid-course corrections, we could go in at 55 hours instead of 58.

Fred Haise @FHLMPilotApollo13
We've just finished eating and cleaning up a bit afterwards. Jim is going around cleaning food debris off all the inlet hoses. I guess we're kind of thinking about getting ready to go to sleep.

One day 13 hours mission time

Vance Brand @VBrandCAPCOM
Sounds like those guys are living it up out there. All that food and music and every 10 minutes getting to look at the Earth and the Moon alternatively.

Fred Haise @FHLMPilotApollo13
It's pretty cloudy down there. About the only land I can see are parts of Australia and Korea. Clouds covering everything else. The Moon is getting bigger but still a ways to go.

Jack Swigert @JSCMPApollo13
Into the pre-sleep checklist now. As far as the crew checklist medication status goes – we've had no medication. We're all feeling fine.

Jack Swigert @JSCMPApollo13
I've given the onboard readouts. Jim is chlorinating the potable water and I'm ready for an E-memory dump. Nearly time for bed.

Vance Brand @VBrandCAPCOM
EECOM says Apollo 13 can go back to AUTO on the hydrogen tank as soon as they stir their cryos. We're now ready to take their E-memory dump.

Vance Brand @VBrandCAPCOM
The spacecraft is in real good shape. We're all bored to tears down here in Mission Control.

Jim Lovell @JLCDRApollo13
We're all going to bed now – after we play our last rendition of 'With Their Eyes On The Stars'.

One day 23 hours mission time

Jim Lovell @JLCDRApollo13
After some good sleep and nine-and-a-half hours off-comms, we're waking up and getting the spacecraft ship-shape again.

Jim Lovell @JLCDRApollo13
Breaking out some breakfast, after which I'll send the flight surgeon our sleep report.

Joe Kerwin @JKerwinCAPCOM
Received Apollo 13's sleep report. Jim had about 5 hours sleep, Jack had 6 hours and Freddo had about 9 hours - Jim had a hard time waking Freddo up.

Jim Lovell @JLCDRApollo13
I just informed Houston of an 'interesting' incident after we went to sleep last night. We had a MASTER ALARM and it really scared us. We were all over the cockpit like wet noodles.

Joe Kerwin @JKerwinCAPCOM
I told Jim I'm sorry the MASTER ALARM didn't amount to anything significant - they could probably do with some excitement up there right now.

Joe Kerwin @JKerwinCAPCOM
Nice music they are listening to now – 'With Their Eyes On The Stars' yet again. I have a hydrogen tank procedure for them to do after they stir up the cryos.

Joe Kerwin @JKerwinCAPCOM
Apollo 13 now has 76% hydrogen and 81% oxygen. However, we show the oxygen No. 2 tank reading off scale. We're pretty sure it's a sensor failure, but we've asked Jim for onboard verification.

Jim Lovell @JLCDRApollo13
Our gauge reading on number 2 oxygen tank is reading off-scale high now as Houston indicated. However, Jack tells me it was okay when he first looked at it this morning.

Joe Kerwin @JKerwinCAPCOM
At 46 hours, 45 minutes we had 82% on number 2 oxygen tank and apparently when Jack stirred the cryos, the sensor broke.

Joe Kerwin @JKerwinCAPCOM
It's no problem. The crew of Apollo 13 are above nominal on all their consumables including oxygen.

Jim Lovell @JLCDRApollo13
Houston has confirmed that the third mid-course correction has been deleted. Fred and I will now enter the lunar module at 55 hours into the flight – about 7 hours from now.

Joe Kerwin @JKerwinCAPCOM
Apollo 13 can crank up for the TV sometime prior to 55 hours at their convenience, just to set it up. We will be expecting broadcast at 55 hours.

Joe Kerwin @JKerwinCAPCOM
We've requested Jim do the oxygen fuel cell purge and waste water dump at 54 hours, 50 minutes.

Joe Kerwin @JKerwinCAPCOM
One other thing we'd like to have the crew do sometime soon is to cycle the cryo fan in number 2 oxygen tank one more time. We'd like to see if we can get that sensor back.

Jack Swigert @JSCMPApollo13
I've switched on the fan on number 2 oxygen tank. It's stirring now.

Joe Kerwin @JKerwinCAPCOM
We're working on amending the procedure for bleeding out the additional nitrogen from the lunar module to ensure the vehicle has the proper oxygen level when they get to the Moon's surface.

Jack Swigert @JSCMPApollo13
Houston have a flight plan update for me to get us into a good position to film Comet Bennet when we are in a position to do so. Should be awesome!

Joe Kerwin @JKerwinCAPCOM
We're ready to have Number 2 oxygen tank fan switched off. Looks like we didn't get the sensor back.

2 days 2 hours mission time

Joe Kerwin @JKerwinCAPCOM
We need Apollo 13 to do a switch conversion on the cryo oxygen tanks. We need them to go to: heaters tank 1 OFF, tank 2 AUTO. That will be the opposite way they've got them now.

Joe Kerwin @JKerwinCAPCOM
I had to issue Jack a correction. My mistake. We mean HYDROGEN tanks. Tank 1 heater to OFF, tank 2 to AUTO.

Jack Swigert @JSCMPApollo13
Our heater configuration is now: hydrogen, Heater 1 – OFF, Heater 2 – AUTO. Both oxygen heaters are in AUTO.

Joe Kerwin @JKerwinCAPCOM
The new heater configurations should keep the astronauts from getting continuous CAUTION AND WARNING lights during their sleep cycle. They'll get them during the day, but that's okay.

Joe Kerwin @JKerwinCAPCOM
I have just read up to Apollo 13 the changes to the lunar module entry procedures they'll be undertaking at 55 hours, and the rationale for the changes.

Fred Haise @FHLMPilotApollo13
We now have the 12 updated, complex technical procedures we need to do to ensure a secure passage from the command vehicle into the lunar module. Far too technical to note down here.

Jim Lovell @JLCDRApollo13
Because of the oxygen tank 2 quantity sensor failure, Houston asked us to keep a closer watch of the cryo quantities.

Jim Lovell @JLCDRApollo13
We're going to have to stir all the tanks at slightly more frequent intervals than had been planned.

Jim Lovell @JLCDRApollo13
We're starting the newly scheduled stir procedures now and will be stirring them every 5 or 6 hours except during sleep and high activity periods.

Jim Lovell @JLCDRApollo13
Each tank will be stirred for the normal one minute or so.

Vance Brand @VBrandCAPCOM
Jim seems in very good spirits. When I told him my prediction on the hydrogen tank CAUTION AND WARNING lights and the light coming on, he asked me if I'd like to go to the horse races with him.

Vance Brand @VBrandCAPCOM
The crew are complaining about the comms signal. Reception has been going in and out and we often have to repeat instructions. It's probably just as a result of them being further out.

Fred Haise @FHLMPilotApollo13
Time for some grits here again. We just ate a can of ham salad. That was quite an experience. It's kind of like eating on the sly… chasing it around.

Jim Lovell @JLCDRApollo13
We're not doing anything right now, so we're wondering if we could start the lunar module entry procedures even earlier than re-scheduled. Houston say they will get back to us on that.

Jim Lovell @JLCDRApollo13
We'd also like to move up the next waste water dump and maybe the oxygen fuel cell purge a little earlier if Houston agrees.

Vance Brand @VBrandCAPCOM
Apollo 13 can start preparing for entry to the lunar module at their leisure. We have also approved an immediate waste water dump and fuel cell purge.

Fred Haise @FHLMPilotApollo13
We are removing the hatch between the command module and the lunar module so I can crawl into the lunar module for a preliminary look around.

Jack Swigert @JSCMPApollo13
We've transferred to lunar module power at 54 hours 46 minutes, well ahead of the initial flight schedule.

Jack Lousma @JLousmaCAPCOM
Apollo 13 are coming in with a lot of background noise. I believe Freddo said the docking tunnel index mark was minus 2 degrees. He is now through step 7 of the lunar module entry procedure.

Jim Lovell @JLCDRApollo13
Connection and lunar module checklist procedure completed and terminated at 54 hours, 58 minutes and 50 seconds. We are now back on command and service module power.

Jim Lovell @JLCDRApollo13
Time to send down some more TV. We'll start by filming through Odyssey, then in through the tunnel to Aquarius and show a little of the inside of lunar module Aquarius.

Jim Lovell @JLCDRApollo13
Freddo, as landing vehicle pilot, will be filmed transporting himself through the tunnel and into Aquarius.

Two days 7 hours mission time

Fred Haise @FHLMPilotApollo13
Orientation is very different here than it was in the simulations in the NASA water tank. I find myself standing with my head on the floor when I enter the lunar module.

Jack Lousma @JLousmaCAPCOM
Those are great pictures coming down now. They've got the light just right.

Jim Lovell @JLCDRApollo13
We're trying to see if Freddo, while he's inside Aquarius, can get some pictures back at the command module.

Jim Lovell @JLCDRApollo13
Freddo is now playing with his second favorite pastime – rigging his hammock for sleep on the lunar surface. His first favorite pastime of course being breaking into the food locker.

Fred Haise @FHLMPilotApollo13
It's pretty difficult getting into a hammock in zero gravity. I'm not sure if I keep floating away from it, or if it keeps floating away from me.

Jim Lovell @JLCDRApollo13
For the benefit of the television viewers, we've just about completed our inspection of lunar module Aquarius, and now we're proceeding through the hatchy-gap back to command module Odyssey.

Jim Lovell @JLCDRApollo13
Fred, Jack and myself have all commented, as have many people in the past, on how much bigger the spacecraft appears in actual flight when you have so much ease in moving compared to the simulator.

Jack Lousma @JLousmaCAPCOM
We're seeing such good pictures right now. It looks like the characters shaved before the show this time.

Jack Lousma @JLousmaCAPCOM
Well, Jack Swigert needs to keep up his TV image - he is the only remaining bachelor among the NASA astronauts.

Jim Lovell @JLCDRApollo13
Our little tape recorder has been a big benefit in passing away some of the time on our transit to the Moon.

Jim Lovell @JLCDRApollo13
It's rather odd to see the tape recorder floating while it's playing the theme from 2001, and of course – the song Aquarius.

Jim Lovell @JLCDRApollo13
We just concluded the TV show, inspection of lunar module Aquarius and wished everyone back on Earth a pleasant evening.

Jim Lovell @JLCDRApollo13
We are now heading back for a pleasant evening ourselves aboard command module Odyssey.

Gene Kranz @GKFlgtDirApollo13
We have one more item for Apollo 13. We'd like them to stir up their cryo tanks at their convenience.

Jack Lousma @JLousmaCAPCOM
We are also sending up some attitude adjustments so the crew can try to get some really good shots of Comet Bennet.

Jack Swigert @JSCMPApollo13
Stirring the cryo tanks now.

Jack Lousma @JLousmaCAPCOM
We're seeing a hardware re-start on our screens down here.

Jack Swigert @JSCMPApollo13
We've had a problem here. We have a MAIN B BUS UNDERVOLT!

Gene Kranz @GKFlgtDirApollo13
Apollo 13 have reported a MAIN B BUS UNDERVOLT. We are looking into the problem. It may be just an instrumentation issue.

Gene Kranz @GKFlgtDirApollo13
However, if it means an actual loss of electrical power on the spacecraft, it could be serious. We're still looking into it.

Fred Haise @FHLMPilotApollo13
The voltage is… looking good, but we had a pretty large bang associated with the CAUTION AND WARNING lamp. While Houston looks at this, we're going ahead and buttoning up the tunnel again.

Jack Lousma @JLousmaCAPCOM
That jolt must have rocked the sensor on number 2 oxygen tank. It was oscillating down around 20 to 60 percent. Now it's fullscale high again.

Fred Haise @FHLMPilotApollo13
We have a MAIN BUS A UNDERVOLT also showing now, and MAIN BUS B is showing zero electrical power.

Jack Lousma @JLousmaCAPCOM
We've asked Apollo 13 to try to reconnect fuel cell 1 to MAIN A, and fuel cell 3 to MAIN B.

Fred Haise @FHLMPilotApollo13
I tried to reset, but fuel cells 1 and 3 are both still showing zero electrical power.

Gene Kranz @GKFlgtDirApollo13
Everyone here at Mission Control is trying to come up with some good ideas for Apollo 13. At this time, we're asking them to open circuit fuel cell 1 and leave 2 and 3 as they are.

Jim Lovell @JLCDRApollo13
Our oxygen number 2 tank is now reading quantity as zero. And it looks to me, looking out the hatch, that we are venting something. We're venting something... into space.

Jack Lousma @JLousmaCAPCOM
We've asked Apollo 13 to do a powerdown until they have a Delta reading of 10 amps less than what they have now.

Fred Haise @FHLMPilotApollo13
Houston tells us they have lots of people working on this and will give us some dope when they get it.

Fred Haise @FHLMPilotApollo13
I'm thinking if we lose all electrical power in the command module, we may have to get into the lunar module.

Gene Kranz @GKFlgtDirApollo13
We've got a good MAIN A electrical bus right now. We have to be sure that whatever we do doesn't screw up MAIN A.

Jack Lousma @JLousmaCAPCOM
Apollo 13 is reporting many more electrical systems going offline right now.

Gene Kranz @GKFlgtDirApollo13
This could be serious, but we need to remain calm and, most of all... methodical.

Gene Kranz @GKFlgtDirApollo13
We need to be looking at this problem from the standpoint of status. We need to figure out what we have on the spacecraft that's good right now.

Jim Lovell @JLCDRApollo13
We are continuing to vent a gas of some sort. Venting it into space. This is not good. Not good at all.

Fred Haise @FHLMPilotApollo13
We are able to see the gas venting into space out of window 1. It's coming out at quite a rate.

Gene Kranz @GKFlgtDirApollo13
We need to call in whatever backup we have available and get some more brainpower on this.

Gene Kranz @GKFlgtDirApollo13
We need to keep cool. We have the lunar module still attached. That vehicle is good so if we need to get back home, we have that vehicle to do a good portion of it with.

Jack Swigert @JSCMPApollo13
Something is messing with our pitch and roll, so I'm suspecting it is whatever is venting back there. I'm trying my best to stabilize the spacecraft.

Gene Kranz @GKFlgtDirApollo13
We need to be sure we don't do anything that will blow our electrical power with the batteries or cause us to lose fuel cell number 2. The best thing we can do right now is go to a powerdown.

Gene Kranz @GKFlgtDirApollo13
We want to keep the oxygen and that kind of stuff working. We're in good shape if we need to get home, so let's solve the problem and not make it any worse by guessing.

Two days 8 hours mission time

Jack Lousma @JLousmaCAPCOM
Apollo 13 have had to power down even more to conserve what power is remaining, including turning down their lights.

Jim Lovell @JLCDRApollo13
I'm transmitting but I don't have any current now. Houston is trying to figure out how to restore power to the oxygen tanks.

Jack Lousma @JLousmaCAPCOM
We'd like to build up the pressure in oxygen tank 1, so Jim needs to turn on the heaters manually and we'll watch the pressure for him.

Jack Swigert @JSCMPApollo13
Looking outside, the number of particles has diminished greatly, almost ceased. Whatever was venting has almost stopped.

Fred Haise @FHLMPilotApollo13
Hydrogen tanks 1 and 2 are reading 230 psi. Oxygen tank 1 is barely holding its own at 300, and oxygen tank 2 is reading zero. Waste water is reading 34, and potable water is reading about 98.

Seymour (Sy) Liebergot

Sy Liebergot was a senior flight controller during the NASA Moon program. During the flight of Apollo 13, he held the position of EECOM, meaning he was responsible for the environmental and electrical systems onboard the spacecraft.

Seymour Liebergot @SyEECOM
Oxygen pressure will hit 100 psi in less than 2 hours from now. If the pressure gets that low, that's the end right there.

Fred Haise @FHLMPilotApollo13
On the DC indicator, fuel cell 1 is reading 0 amps and fuel cell 2 is oscillating between 44 and 48 amps depending on thruster activity.

Jack Swigert @JSCMPApollo13
I have no negative pitch control of the spacecraft right now. I have got a positive pitch rate and I can't stop it.

Seymour Liebergot @SyEECOM
It appears Apollo 13 is losing oxygen flow through fuel cell 3. We need them to close the valve on fuel cell 3.

Seymour Liebergot @SyEECOM
Also, they should turn off the inline heaters on fuel cell 1 and go through the shutdown procedures on fuel cell 3.

Seymour Liebergot @SyEECOM
This could mean aborting the mission.

Jack Swigert @JSCMPApollo13
Houston helped me out on the pitch control. I've got it back now.

Fred Haise @FHLMPilotApollo13
Oxygen tank number 1 pressure is less than 300 now.

Jack Lousma @JLousmaCAPCOM
We have confirmed the sharp drop in oxygen pressure and note that this is also indicated by the reduction in temperature.

Jack Swigert @JSCMPApollo13
We're proceeding on the shutdown procedure for fuel cell 1.

Gene Kranz @GKFlgtDirApollo13
Shutting down those fuel cells effectively rules out the Moon landing. We are now in full-on recovery mode.

Gene Kranz @GKFlgtDirApollo13
All of our return to Earth planning right now should be assuming we are using the lunar module for all maneuvering from this point forward, around the Moon and back to re-entry interface.

Jack Swigert @JSCMPApollo13
Oxygen tank 1 pressure is now barely a hair above 200. It's slowly going down to zero and we're thinking about going into the lunar module to use it as a 'lifeboat'.

Jack Lousma @JLousmaCAPCOM
We at Mission Control are also thinking of using the lunar module as a lifeboat. We're talking it over and are preparing procedures which will allow the astronauts to use the lunar module's systems and consumables.

Gene Kranz @GKFlgtDirApollo13
Right now, we need to know the minimum power levels we will need in the lunar module – the minimum needed to sustain life.

Gene Kranz @GKFlgtDirApollo13
I'm handing over flight control to Glynn and his black team now. Hopefully, fresh minds will get a good handle on this.

Gene Kranz @GKFlgtDirApollo13
I'm assuming Glynn and his team are pretty much briefed and up to speed as best they can be at this point.

Gene Kranz @GKFlgtDirApollo13
My team will go over the logs and try to figure out what happened in the service module while Glynn's fresh team keep on top of things real time.

2 days 9 hours mission time

Glynn S. Lunney @GKFlgtDirApollo13
We need to be figuring out every possible thing we can do without to conserve even more power on the spacecraft right now.

Glynn S. Lunney @GKFlgtDirApollo13
We don't anticipate an immediate emergency evacuation into the lunar module. The crew should be able to stay in the command module for a while longer while we work on stuff down here.

Jack Swigert @JSCMPApollo13
We've turned off the waste heaters to conserve more power. If we are going to do another waste water dump, it might be best to do it now while the duct is still warm there.

Glynn S. Lunney @GKFlgtDirApollo13
It will save a little more power if we can turn the high-gain antenna off and just work off of the big dish.

Jack Swigert @JSCMPApollo13
Freddo and Jim are making their way through the hatch into the lunar module. Freddo should have power on in the 'lifeboat' momentarily.

BREAKING NEWS
Jules Bergman @JBABCNews
The command module of Apollo 13 has apparently lost nearly all electrical power and the three astronauts are now making their way into the lunar module to use it as a lifeboat.

Jules Bergman @JBABCNews
The astronauts are also said to be losing breathing oxygen. The emergency has ruled out any possibility of a lunar landing. The mission now is to bring the astronauts home safely.

Glynn S. Lunney @GKFlgtDirApollo13
We need Apollo 13 to verify that all the fuel cell pumps are off, and have them turn off the oxygen fans in tank number 2.

Jack Lousma @JLousmaCAPCOM
Oxygen pressure is now 217 psi... still coming down.

Jack Swigert @JSCMPApollo13
Oxygen tank number 2 fans are now off. That leaves me with just tank number 1 fans on and tank number 1 heaters on.

Jack Lousma @JLousmaCAPCOM
We're now in communication with Freddo who is in Aquarius – what may become the lunar module lifeboat.

Glynn S. Lunney

Lunney seated at his console in Mission Control

Glynn Lunney was a NASA engineer and flight director. He had worked for NASA since the very beginning in 1958, acting as flight director during both the Gemini and Apollo programs. During the Apollo 13 crisis, Lunney and his team came on shift just over an hour after the explosion in the service module and had to figure out how to power up the lunar module in an unprecedented amount of time and before the pressure in the oxygen tanks fell so low that the astronauts would run out of breathable air.

Glynn S. Lunney @GKFlgtDirApollo13
Just got a very serious update from EECOM. Looks like we've got only about 18 minutes before we get down to 100 psi on the oxygen and that's sort of the cut-off point.

Jim Lovell @JLCDRApollo13
We have gone through a huge amount of detailed procedures in both Odyssey and Aquarius in the past 5 minutes and Houston is relaying even more as I type.

Glynn S. Lunney @GKFlgtDirApollo13
We now figure there is only about 15 minutes' worth of electrical power left in the command module. The crew need to start getting everything over to the lunar module and getting some power in there sharpish.

Glynn S. Lunney @GKFlgtDirApollo13
One thing we must not do at this point while we are desperately searching for electrical power is draw off power from the re-entry batteries in Odyssey. If we do that, the crew won't get back.

Glynn S. Lunney @GKFlgtDirApollo13
The crew are going to have to be living out of lunar module Aquarius from here on in. All three astronauts need to get in there within the next 10 minutes and have everything powered up.

Jim Lovell @JLCDRApollo13
Looks like we've lost the Moon for sure. The mission now is to find a way to get back to Earth.

Jack Swigert @JSCMPApollo13
I just got a MASTER ALARM and Main Bus A Undervolt. I'm starting to power down now.

Jack Swigert @JSCMPApollo13
I'm powering down the inertial measurement unit. I have no control at all and am going to turn off my 16 jets. Oxygen and fans are off in tank 1.

Fred Haise @FHLMPilotApollo13
We've opened up the suit flow valves and have air flowing in the lunar module now.

Jim Lovell @JLCDRApollo13
The command module Odyssey is now almost completely powered down.

Jack Lousma @JLousmaCAPCOM
I've asked Apollo 13 again to let us know when they have attitude control in the lunar module.

Glynn S. Lunney @GKFlgtDirApollo13
All fuel cell pumps are now off. No need for them any more since there is nothing left that can be pumped. Same with the fans in oxygen tank 2.

Fred Haise @FHLMPilotApollo13
I'm still working on pressurizing the lunar module with some much-needed help from the command module.

Jack Swigert @JSCMPApollo13
I'm currently communicating simultaneously with Freddo who is in the lunar module with me, Jack back at Mission Control, Houston and Jim the command module. It's all getting a little frantic.

Glynn S. Lunney @GKFlgtDirApollo13
We're getting a huge amount of noise on the comms right now, which is not exactly helping matters.

Jack Lousma @JLousmaCAPCOM
We need the crew to try their best to hold their present attitude of Odyssey and Aquarius until the lunar module gets powered up.

Jack Lousma @JLousmaCAPCOM
Fred and Jack are both speaking at once. We need just one at a time if we're going to get this mess sorted out and have a chance of bringing these men home.

Jack Swigert @JSCMPApollo13
I'm going to try to fly according to the lunar terminator - the line of shadow across the Moon's surface.

Glynn S. Lunney @GKFlgtDirApollo13
Odyssey needs to coordinate with Aquarius on attitude control.

Jim Lovell @JLCDRApollo13
I can't tell if Jack is firing anything. He says he "doesn't think" he is.

Jim Lovell @JLCDRApollo13
After the latest procedures Houston sent up, we have established attitude control in the lunar module now. We're going to try to rotate up and see how that goes.

Illustration: Fred Haise and Jim Lovell are in the lunar module (left). Jack Swigert is in the command module.

Glynn S. Lunney @GKFlgtDirApollo13
We have attitude control in the lunar module confirmed by Jim now, so we are moving forward... one step at a time. Good job everyone!

Walter Cronkite @WCronkiteCBSNews
The flight of Apollo 13 is in serious jeopardy this morning.

Walter Cronkite @WCronkiteCBSNews
As the spaceship was some 205,000 miles from Earth, speeding towards the Moon, the fuel cells that supply it with electrical power suddenly failed.

Walter Cronkite @WCronkiteCBSNews
With this lack of power, the Moon landing could not be completed and it is now a question of getting the men home safely.

Walter Cronkite @WCronkiteCBSNews
That can be done by using the engines of the lunar module to power and steer all 3 stages of the spacecraft—a procedure never before attempted.

Walter Cronkite @WCronkiteCBSNews
This is indeed the gravest emergency yet in the history of the American space program. The whole circumstance began unfolding at around 10 o'clock EST—some 3 hours ago.

Jules Bergman @JBABCNews
As things stand now, with what we are hearing from NASA, it appears there is less than a 10% chance of bringing the Apollo 13 astronauts home.

Walter Cronkite @WCronkiteCBSNews
The Apollo 13 command module has 3 fuel cells. 1 and 3 went out almost immediately and cell no. 2 began draining rapidly.

Walter Cronkite @WCronkiteCBSNews
To try to conserve power in that fuel cell, they shut down all power and went on to use battery power from the lunar module landing vehicle Aquarius.

Walter Cronkite @WCronkiteCBSNews
With the power down, the astronauts are no longer able to determine their exact attitude through their instruments, but are navigating by simply viewing out of the window the terminator—the Sun's line of shadow across the Moon.

Wally Schirra @WSchirraNASA
As well as using the Moon, NASA is looking at the star pattern (the celestial sphere as we call it) to determine which navigation stars are available.

Wally Schirra @WSchirraNASA
We have 37 navigation stars that can be picked up out of the window.

Wally Schirra @WSchirraNASA
A crude attitude can be determined initially using the stars. The reason they need a fairly precise determination of their attitude is because they have to fire their engines soon.

Wally Schirra @WSchirraNASA
The next alignment will be a 'fine alignment'. If the attitude is in the wrong direction, the burn will take them off in the wrong direction and they could end up plowing into the Moon.

Glynn S. Lunney @GKFlgtDirApollo13
The emergency procedures are going fairly well. Odyssey is now powered down and we are getting good data from Aquarius.

Fred Haise @FHLMPilotApollo13
Houston asked me if I can see any stars out of the lunar module window. That would be a help with alignment calculations. Unfortunately, the windows are coated with water right now.

Glynn S. Lunney @GKFlgtDirApollo13
We have a new problem now. With the command module now completely powered down we have lost all reliable tracking data. We're going to have to figure out a new way of tracking the spacecraft.

Glynn S. Lunney @GKFlgtDirApollo13
EECOM tells me the tracking data from the lunar module is no good. That's one major problem. Also, we need to work on the long-range 'lifeboat problems' associated with Aquarius.

Glynn S. Lunney @GKFlgtDirApollo13
When Freddo has wiped off the lunar module's windows, we're ready to crank up some lunar module simulations to correlate with what constellations and stars he can identify out of his windows.

Jim Lovell @JLCDRApollo13
I'm looking out of Freddo's window. I can see a lot of particles and they're all drifting away from us. I don't recognize any constellations right now in this particular attitude.

Glynn S. Lunney @GKFlgtDirApollo13
I'm asking everyone around the room here in Mission Control to try real hard to figure out whatever they can to save more current on the spacecraft. If we can't, we are not going to be able to bring those guys home.

Two days 11 hours mission time

Glynn S. Lunney @GKFlgtDirApollo13
We have some procedures to upload now to power down the displays in the spacecraft. They won't save a lot of current, but every little helps at this point.

Fred Haise @FHLMPilotApollo13
Why the hell are we maneuvering at all now? Are we still venting stuff out into space?

Roy Neal @RNealCBSNews
The return to Earth will not begin until the lunar module is in the correct attitude and the lunar module engine is fired to accelerate the spacecraft so that it will go quickly around the Moon and then return to Earth.

Walter Cronkite @WCronkiteCBSNews
Using the lunar module Aquarius engine for the burn is possible because that engine gets its power from storage batteries - not fuel cells like those in the service module that power the command module Odyssey.

Jim Lovell @JLCDRApollo13
Houston has just told us that if we can pull this off, they expect to have us splashing down in the Atlantic at 133 hours mission time. That was good to hear I guess.

Glynn S. Lunney @GKFlgtDirApollo13
An Atlantic landing is not optimal given the darkness and lack of recovery ships in that location at that time, but it's the best we can do if we have to opt for the most rapid return possible.

Vance Brand @VBrandCAPCOM
Apollo 13 have the computer again. No more maneuvering will be needed until the burn. They can just sit in the burn attitude until then.

Jim Lovell @JLCDRApollo13
We just had another PROGRAM ALARM go off. Turned out to be nothing much, but it's getting very tense in here.

Jim Lovell @JLCDRApollo13
We must be getting pretty close to the Moon now. Pity it's just going to be another fly by - I've already done one of those.

Jim Lovell @JLCDRApollo13
All of us should get a good look at the Moon as we fly by – it's likely to be some time before NASA launches another Moon mission after this failure.

View from Aquarius of the Moon and its terminator (line of shadow)

Glynn S. Lunney @GKFlgtDirApollo13
Right now, we don't have tracking on the spacecraft. We're doing everything we can to establish that somehow, but it was never figured we'd have to do it with a powered down command module.

Jim Lovell @JLCDRApollo13
The next thing is power up for the burn. We need Houston to give us the time for the power up.

Glynn S. Lunney @GKFlgtDirApollo13
We'll send up the burn procedures shortly - after the crew have finished eating.

Glynn S. Lunney @GKFlgtDirApollo13
We need to know if we can get the crew all the way home with 25 amps on the lunar module. EECOM is

telling me no... we need to get down to 15 amps or so.

Glynn S. Lunney @GKFlgtDirApollo13
We also need to be looking at the CO_2 scrubbing levels which will become critical very shortly. Closest approach to the Moon is still estimated to be at about 60 miles.

Walter Cronkite @WCronkiteCBSNews
Right now aboard the spacecraft, the men are setting power levels.

Walter Cronkite @WCronkiteCBSNews
At Mission Control, Houston, the various support sections are figuring out what power levels they can operate with the limited amount of battery power available from Aquarius.

Glynn S. Lunney @GKFlgtDirApollo13
We're going to cut off contact with Apollo 13 for about 25 seconds while we try to re-establish tracking. Right now, we don't have tracking.

Jim Lovell @JLCDRApollo13
In order to save even more power, we're thinking of rigging up the urine dump to the side hatch to save urine heater power. Every little helps at this point.

THE TIMES
Apollo crew take emergency steps for return to earth

'Most serious situation we have ever faced in space'
Power and oxygen run short

Glynn S. Lunney @GKFlgtDirApollo13
We now have the Apollo 13 backup crew installed in the simulator looking at some docked burns and trying to see what kind of alignment procedures they can come up with by looking out of the windows of Aquarius.

Jim Lovell @JLCDRApollo13
We're not able to see any stars right now. The sunlight is reflecting off the thrusters and the debris that came away at the time of the mishap is still with us, such that the stars are hard to find.

Glynn S. Lunney @GKFlgtDirApollo13
If Jim can orient the lunar module so the service module would be between them and the Sun, we believe the crew would be able to see and recognize constellations out of their front windows.

Glynn S. Lunney @GKFlgtDirApollo13
EECOM has just told me the crew will run out of water in 34 hours.

Fred Haise @FHLMPilotApollo13
We're getting really bad static on the communications from Mission Control now. Really

hard to hear. The last thing we need is to be cut off from Houston at this point.

Fred Haise @FHLMPilotApollo13
Every time Houston transmits, the static level goes way up making it impossible to hear.

Glynn S. Lunney @GKFlgtDirApollo13
We are now looking at taking offline the computer, guidance system, cabin heater, docking radar, landing radar, instrument panel displays and dozens of other smaller items.

Glynn S. Lunney @GKFlgtDirApollo13
Hopefully, all of those needed systems can be powered up again shortly before re-entry... if they haven't frozen solid by that time that is.

Glynn S. Lunney @GKFlgtDirApollo13
Figuring out the detailed procedures for powering up the command module needs to be done in less than 3 days. Three days to complete work we usually spend 3 months on!

Jim Lovell @JLCDRApollo13
Just made out only one clear word from Houston. It could be my pitch attitude that is breaking up the incoming signal, but it seems like they are hearing us.

Fred Haise @FHLMPilotApollo13
So close to the Moon now, but all we are concerned about now is getting around there and shooting off back to Earth.

Fred Haise @FHLMPilotApollo13
I had been hoping to get much closer to the Moon than 60 miles. I had hoped and trained for years to be kicking up some dust and hopping around with Jim down there. Damn!

Two days 12 hours mission time

Jack Lousma @JLousmaCAPCOM
We're working hard on fixing the comms signals between Earth and Apollo 13. Hoping to get the crew to see the constellations from their windows. It was very helpful during Apollo 10.

Jim Lovell @JLCDRApollo13
Finally getting a clear signal coming up from Mission Control. Hope it stays this time. We really need the help of those guys down there in Houston.

Glynn S. Lunney @GKFlgtDirApollo13
We're going to have the crew do a 16-foot-per-second course correction burn 37 minutes from now.

Glynn S. Lunney @GKFlgtDirApollo13
Water is a critical issue in the lunar module right now. We need them to use as little as possible.

Walter Cronkite @WCronkiteCBSNews
One of the main concerns right now of the technicians at Mission Control is the level of what they call 'consumables'. That is, the water, food, oxygen and electrical power available to the astronauts.

Wally Schirra @WSchirraNASA
Much of the water needed by Apollo astronauts is produced as a by-product from the fuel cells. There

is also water in the lunar module, stored there for the crew.

Wally Schirra @WSchirraNASA
I'm not worried about water or food. It's power and breathable air for the crew that are the concern right now. Currently, the command and service modules are powered down completely.

Jack Lousma @JLousmaCAPCOM
We have no communication at all between us and the spacecraft available right now. A lot of guys are working on it down here.

Wally Schirra @WSchirraNASA
The combined 'stack' of the spacecraft is now rolling around the different attitudes and it seems Jim Lovell is having difficulty controlling the thrusters on the lunar module to maneuver the entire stack.

Wally Schirra @WSchirraNASA
Those thrusters were only intended to maneuver the lunar module during the descent stage as a single unit. Not when the lunar module is combined with both the command module and service module.

Wally Schirra @WSchirraNASA
Jim will be going through a new and steep learning curve right now. Those thrusters and the lunar module are off-center from the center of mass of the entire stack.

Wally Schirra @WSchirraNASA
This is a very difficult set of procedures Jim is having to learn on the fly out in space and not in a simulator on Earth.

Walter Cronkite @WCronkiteCBSNews
I've heard some people at NASA say that Jack Swigert is the best man to have on board right now since he "wrote the book" on the command module and all the things that can go wrong with it.

Glynn S. Lunney @GKFlgtDirApollo13
We have a procedure to send up that we think might solve the comms problem. The problem right now is we can't talk to the crew to pass up the procedure.

Jim Lovell @JLCDRApollo13
We need more time to prepare for the burn. Houston had it scheduled it for 61 hours, 30 minutes.

Walter Cronkite @WCronkiteCBSNews
So another critical maneuver is coming up. That descent propulsion system engine is throttleable—that is, it can be operated from 1,050 pounds thrust to 9,500 pounds thrust.

Wally Schirra @WSchirraNASA
If Houston is not able to re-establish communications with the spacecraft, the detailed procedures for the course correction burn can not be sent up to the crew.

Walter Cronkite @WCronkiteCBSNews
They really don't need much of a burn at this point, just enough to increase their speed 14 and a half miles an hour.

Walter Cronkite @WCronkiteCBSNews
That burn will give them the speed to get them back on a so-called 'free-return trajectory' around the Moon.

Walter Cronkite @WCronkiteCBSNews
That slight increase in speed will ensure that they don't go skimming around the Moon and put them on a track to return safely to Earth.

Jack Lousma @JLousmaCAPCOM
Still out of touch with Apollo 13. All we're getting is static right now. I'll keep trying.

Jim Lovell @JLCDRApollo13
We're not able to see the stars to help us in our alignment and navigation, but we are able to see the Earth and Moon. That may be enough if we can figure out how to do it.

Jack Lousma @JLousmaCAPCOM
OK, we're back in touch... barely. A huge amount of background noise and static coming down from Apollo 13 right now.

Fred Haise @FHLMPilotApollo13
I'm looking out of the right window and seeing a thousand or so false stars out there – left over from some of the debris from the accident. It's hard to discern what's real and what's not real.

Glynn S. Lunney @GKFlgtDirApollo13
We lost touch with the crew again. If we can get it back, we can complete sending up procedures for a 16ft/second burn to put them on a free return trajectory around the Moon.

Jim Lovell @JLCDRApollo13
We're about to conduct a test with the lunar module's thrusters to see if we can establish enough control and guidance to enable Aquarius to

maneuver itself and the attached command module as one spaceship.

Glynn S. Lunney @GKFlgtDirApollo13
Okay, we have re-established communications with the spacecraft. Everyone needs to stay quiet right now... we have a lot of business to do.

Jim Lovell @JLCDRApollo13
We are going to do both manual and AUTO maneuvers to alter our attitude and see which works. Houston should be able to monitor the resulting attitude.

Glynn S. Lunney @GKFlgtDirApollo13
We are now water-critical in the lunar module and have asked the crew to use as little as possible. Free return burn could be 37 minutes from now.

Glynn S. Lunney @GKFlgtDirApollo13
We're asking Jim if he's comfortable with doing a 16 ft/second burn 36 minutes from now. He's asked for 15 minutes to go over it and we'll see if he has any other suggestions.

Glynn S. Lunney @GKFlgtDirApollo13
Any suggestions from Jim would be most welcome down here. We can figure out a free return maneuver for any time he wants to give us.

Jim Lovell @JLCDRApollo13
We've gone over the numbers and are asking Houston to approve a free return burn a little later - at 61 hours 25 minutes.

Jim Lovell @JLCDRApollo13
Houston is now suggesting 61 hours 31 minutes to start the free return burn. A little more time is good – this has to be done exactly right.

Glynn S. Lunney @GKFlgtDirApollo13
We need to go through some more alignment procedures and are asking the crew to look out of the windows again to see if they can recognize any constellations or individual stars.

Jim Lovell @JLCDRApollo13
At this attitude, I am not able to see any stars at all. The command module structure is just radiating too much light into the telescope.

Fred Haise @FHLMPilotApollo13
From my windows, one side is totally dark and through the other side I can see thousands of tiny 'stars' which is the debris left over from the explosion. Impossible to say what are real stars and what are not.

Glynn S. Lunney @GKFlgtDirApollo13
Looks like we need to forget about locating stars right now and concentrate on this upcoming free return burn with whatever they are able to see.

Glynn S. Lunney @GKFlgtDirApollo13
Before we initiate the burn, we need to deploy the lunar module landing gear so we don't have any control problems.

Fred Haise @FHLMPilotApollo13
About halfway through the checklist procedures now, page by page. I am now deploying the landing gear on lunar module Aquarius.

Glynn S. Lunney @GKFlgtDirApollo13
Landing gear is now down and locked. We worked through page 11 of the procedures with Freddo and deleted the steps on page 12. Page 13 is done. On to page 14.

Glynn S. Lunney @GKFlgtDirApollo13
15 minutes to the burn and Freddo has worked through page 18 of the procedures. I don't know if we can do/not do the burn if I don't get a consensus GO/NO-GO on this. Hoping for a unanimous GO from the room.

Walter Cronkite @WCronkiteCBSNews
We are listening to Houston confirming with the crew of Apollo 13 that they are instituting all of the procedures for the firing of the descent propulsion engine, now just three and a half minutes away.

Jim Lovell @JLCDRApollo13
It is doubtful whether we'll be able to see the stars in this new configuration. The only way we can possibly get an alignment is with the Earth and its terminator or the Moon and its terminator.

Glynn S. Lunney @GKFlgtDirApollo13
We need to get throttle control to MANUAL. They're still in AUTO right now. Switching to MANUAL should have been done during page 17 read-up procedures.

Glynn S. Lunney @GKFlgtDirApollo13
Throttle control has now been set to MANUAL. Most of the room now reporting we are GO for the burn. Still waiting to hear from M.I.T.

Glynn S. Lunney @GKFlgtDirApollo13
Consensus here at Mission Control now is that we GO for the burn and that it will work. So that is what we will do.

Walter Cronkite @WCronkiteCBSNews
Waiting to hear now from that free return burn due in about a minute and a half from now.

Glynn S. Lunney @GKFlgtDirApollo13
We are recommending Aquarius go to AUTO now, let the thrusters fire, settle down and proceed with the free return burn.

Jack Lousma @JLousmaCAPCOM
Aquarius is GO for the burn.

Jim Lovell @JLCDRApollo13
Burning at 20%... 40%...

Glynn S. Lunney @GKFlgtDirApollo13
Aquarius is looking good.

Jim Lovell @JLCDRApollo13
60%... 80%...

Glynn S. Lunney @GKFlgtDirApollo13
Still looking good.

Jack Lousma @JLousmaCAPCOM
Looked real good. Jim has confirmed AUTO shutdown. No trim required.

Wally Schirra @WSchirraNASA
They've completed the burn. I heard "Apollo shutdown".

Walter Cronkite @WCronkiteCBSNews
They're standing up behind their consoles in Mission Control for a little stretch right now.

Walter Cronkite @WCronkiteCBSNews
The tension of the last several hours is beginning to show. They're standing up and stretching now they've got that critical burn out of the way.

Walter Cronkite @WCronkiteCBSNews
The spaceship is still on its way out to the Moon. But the speed and course should be correct for their flip around the Moon and free return home tomorrow night.

Walter Cronkite @WCronkiteCBSNews
We might point out again why they didn't just turn around and come home. It's not that simple.

Walter Cronkite @WCronkiteCBSNews
It takes a lot of power to stop the flight path they were on. They don't have that power - that's just the trouble.

Wally Schirra @WSchirraNASA
It's possible they could have used the service module engine to turn the craft around, and this was considered.

Wally Schirra @WSchirraNASA
However, it was decided that there was a good chance that engine had been damaged in the explosion and firing it could risk a catastrophe.

Glynn S. Lunney @GKFlgtDirApollo13
Now we're through that burn, we need to go ahead and get as many high-power items offline as we can.

Power conservation is going to be the name of the game for much of the rest of this mission.

Glynn S. Lunney @GKFlgtDirApollo13
Also, really tricky, improvised maneuvering using only the lunar module thrusters and navigating via the stars and the lunar terminator.

Glynn S. Lunney @GKFlgtDirApollo13
We need some quiet in the room – it's getting awful noisy in here. A lot of discussion about the wisdom, or not, of taking Apollo 13's computer offline to save power.

2 days 14 hours mission time

Walter Cronkite @WCronkiteCBSNews
We are waiting now for the Apollo 13 spacecraft to lose contact as it goes behind the Moon. That happens at 7.21 EST and the trip around the far side of the Moon is expected to take around 25 minutes.

Walter Cronkite @WCronkiteCBSNews
After Apollo 13 emerges from behind the Moon, the astronauts will get ready for another firing of their lunar module rocket engine. This burn is expected to increase their speed and lead to a landing in the Pacific on Friday.

Walter Cronkite @WCronkiteCBSNews
The main objective now is to save every possible amount of oxygen, electricity and water. Supplies are adequate for the crippled spacecraft and its crew, but only adequate if there are no delays in bringing them home.

Walter Cronkite @WCronkiteCBSNews
There are still many dangerous hours ahead and everyone at Mission Control, indeed around the nation, is breathing very quietly today.

Gene Kranz @GKFlgtDirApollo13
We're now considering a landing in the Atlantic Ocean at 152 hours 2 minutes flight time. We already have some recovery assets heading there.

Walter Cronkite @WCronkiteCBSNews
We are about to go to Houston where we understand NASA is about to hold a news conference.

James McDivitt @JMManagerApolloProgram
The crew will continue living and moving between Aquarius and Odyssey until sometime before they return when they will return to the command module, put the hatch back and jettison the service module and Aquarius.

James McDivitt @JMManagerApolloProgram
We are searching for 'ships of opportunity' should we have to bring the down into the Atlantic Ocean as seems likely now. The U.S. Navy recovery vessels planned to pick up the astronauts are currently stationed in the Pacific Ocean.

James McDivitt @JMManagerApolloProgram
We don't have a U.S. Navy recovery ship in the Atlantic. If Apollo 13 splashes down in that ocean, the recovery of the astronauts will have to be carried out by a merchant ship, possibly a foreign carrier.

James McDivitt @JMManagerApolloProgram
We have little clue so far as to what happened on Apollo 13, but something pretty violent seems to have happened in bay 4.

James McDivitt @JMManagerApolloProgram
Something happened in the fuel cells and the oxygen tanks. But what exactly happened, I have no idea.

Sigurd Sjoberg @SSDirFlghtOps
In the press conference today, I could not rule out the possibility that Apollo 13 was struck by a meteor. Such an impact would be quite violent and what Apollo 13 suffered was indeed quite violent.

Sigurd Sjoberg @SSDirFlghtOps
If it turns out that we need to land in the Atlantic Ocean, we will consider always having a backup recovery fleet in the Atlantic, not just the Pacific.

Sigurd Sjoberg @SSDirFlghtOps
Right now, we are surveying the Atlantic to see what ships are available.

James McDivitt @JMManagerApolloProgram
The only reason we would go for the Atlantic rather than the Pacific would be if something were to happen between now and the burn to make getting back time-critical.

James McDivitt @JMManagerApolloProgram
An Atlantic landing could get the astronauts back some 9 hours earlier.

Sigurd Sjoberg @SSDirFlghtOps
We're just speculating at the moment, but there are any number of things that could have caused this

explosion. There are several pressurized systems in the service module that could have let go.

Sigurd Sjoberg @SSDirFlghtOps
There's pressurized hydrogen, nitrogen, oxygen. There are fuel cells. It's a very complicated bay there in the service module.

Sigurd Sjoberg @SSDirFlghtOps
The command module is completely powered down and dark right now. When the crew work in there, they have to do so using flashlights. We don't want to use any precious electrical power on systems that are not essential right now.

James McDivitt @JMManagerApolloProgram
We will make every effort to analyze every piece of data to find out what caused the accident, but right now we are putting every effort into bringing our guys home safely. That is what has all of our attention right now.

Sigurd Sjoberg @SSDirFlghtOps
The service module is pretty much useless now since the oxygen is depleted. We do have some propulsion left and the batteries in the lunar module.

Sigurd Sjoberg @SSDirFlghtOps
Initially, we were trying to find out what was wrong in the service module and try and fix it before we lost the oxygen. We weren't able to do that in time.

Sigurd Sjoberg @SSDirFlghtOps
Right now we're concentrating on ensuring we have enough systems to keep the guys alive and bring them home.

James McDivitt @JMManagerApolloProgram
The next burn to get the spacecraft on the correct return to Earth trajectory may take place on the far side of the Moon and will be about 20 to 40 feet per second.

James McDivitt @JMManagerApolloProgram
However, there is still some possibility that we will conduct the burn while still in radio contact.

Fred Haise @FHLMPilotApollo13
Houston just told us we'll have final maneuver updates sent to us at 178 hours flight time. I truly hope they meant 78 hours... 178 hours would be a full day after we're supposed to be splashing down.

Jim Lovell @JLCDRApollo13
We're in the shadow of the Moon now. The Sun is just about set as far as I can see and the stars are all coming out. It's quite a sight!

Jack Swigert @JSCMPApollo13
Passing over the Moon now. So close we can identify even the smaller craters and mountains with the naked eye. Beautiful! So sad Jim and Fred have missed their chance to walk around down there.

View from Aquarius as it passes over the surface of the Moon

Jim Lovell @JLCDRApollo13
I can even see Mount Marilyn from here (named by yours truly). Took time out to snap a few pics to take home with me to show Marilyn... hopefully.

Jim Lovell @JLCDRApollo13
We need to get the cameras squared away now and prepare for the next power up and burn. We're only going to get one chance at this.

James McDivitt @JMManagerApolloProgram
We believe we have a good chance of returning the crew safely. There are many things that could go wrong in the lunar module under stress as it is, such as a loss in electrical power or oxygen, but we are monitoring those closely.

James McDivitt @JMManagerApolloProgram
At the press conference, one of the reporters put me on the spot and I had to answer honestly that this is the most serious situation we have ever had in manned space flight.

James McDivitt @JMManagerApolloProgram
I had to agree that if the accident had happened on the return journey, with the lunar module no longer attached and able to act as a lifeboat, this accident would have almost certainly been fatal to the crew.

Vance Brand @VBrandCAPCOM
Power up and next burn should be in 1 hour and 15 minutes from now.

Jack Swigert @JSCMPApollo13
Houston just told us that the seismometer that was left on the Moon by Apollo 12 picked up a strong impact reading from our Saturn rocket booster as we passed over the Moon's surface. Glad something worked on this flight.

Jim Lovell @JLCDRApollo13
Looking out of the window now, but the Sun is so bright that it's difficult to establish any night vision and we've still got particles floating around us. I'll take a long look and see if I can see any star patterns.

Jack Lousma @JLousmaCAPCOM
I've told Apollo 13 to turn off the transmitter/receiver for 5 minutes. We'll be out of communication for that length of time, but they need to conserve all the power they can.

Jack Lousma @JLousmaCAPCOM
We're looking real close at water usage profiles. Also, we'll recommend for sleeping that the crew leave one guy on watch at all times.

Gene Kranz @GKFlgtDirApollo13
They should avoid making any more urine dumps as they only make the debris problem worse. They need to transfer the following items into Aquarius: some towels, some penlights and fecal bags.

Jim Lovell @JLCDRApollo13
We need Houston to figure out exactly when the next burn needs to be. I've got to figure out a watch schedule and sleep schedule and just how we can meet the next maneuver.

Jack Lousma @JLousmaCAPCOM
Jim will have to maneuver the spacecraft using the lunar module's hand controller in direct mode.

Jack Lousma @JLousmaCAPCOM
We are suggesting that Freddo rest while Jim and Jack are awake. Freddo should hit the sack at about 63 hours, coming up in 25 minutes, and rest for 6 hours.

Jack Lousma @JLousmaCAPCOM
At 70 hours, Jim and Jack should sleep for 6 hours until 76 hours. Ignition time for the next burn will be 79 hours, 25 minutes, 26 and a half seconds.

Fred Haise @FHLMPilotApollo13
Jim and Jack will eat while I sleep. I'm to wake up at 69 hours, after which Jim and Jack will sleep for 6 hours. We are all to eat at 81 to 82 hours, after the next burn.

Jack Lousma @JLousmaCAPCOM
Just sent up a minor modification to the sleep/eat schedule. Jim and Jack ought to eat at 68 to 69 hours.

Jack Lousma @JLousmaCAPCOM
Fred should eat between 69 and 70 hours, just after he wakes up. We have left an hour in there when everybody is awake to talk things over.

Wally Schirra @WSchirraNASA
One of the things people ask us astronauts about is if we have fear in crisis situations. Well, you can't, and we're trained that way.

Wally Schirra @WSchirraNASA
If you allow yourself the luxury of fear, you then open yourself up to the luxury of panic. And panic does nobody any good.

Walter Cronkite @WCronkiteCBSNews
The NASA spokesmen say that the malfunction apparently occurred in the bay which includes the hydrogen tanks, the oxygen tanks and the fuel cells, and was in no way connected with anything that happened in the command module.

Deke Slayton @DKDrctrFlghtCrwOps
We've run a fairly thorough analysis and found a couple of minor adjustments that will save them 1 amp and a little water. We'll send up the details after the crew have rested a little.

Walter Cronkite @WCronkiteCBSNews
They expect to be able to power the command module from the lunar module at low power levels

through the wiring which is normally used to power the LEM from the command module.

Walter Cronkite @WCronkiteCBSNews
So they expect to be using a dual-spacecraft mode from now until the time the spacecraft gets back to Earth.

Gene Kranz @GKFlgtDirApollo13
We're starting to think about the carbon dioxide buildup in the command module and recommend taking Jim's hoses in the lunar module and have them figure out a way to fasten the hoses so they blow into Odyssey.

Jim Lovell @JLCDRApollo13
I'm trying to extend the hose through the tunnel into the command module so it will blow and circulate up and around Odyssey and keep the carbon dioxide level down.

Jack Swigert @JSCMPApollo13
Houston is recommending that we momentarily pressurize the surge tank, drain out all the water until we can't get any more water out of it and store the water in little bags. This, in order to conserve oxygen.

Jack Lousma @JLousmaCAPCOM
Getting a lot of static and other noise again right now. It's becoming more and more difficult to communicate detailed instructions to the Apollo 13 crew.

Jim Lovell @JLCDRApollo13
Houston is asking us to speak slowly and loudly due to all the background noise they're getting. We're getting a lot of the noise too.

Jack Lousma @JLousmaCAPCOM
We need Jim to let us know when he completes his first 90 degree yaw maneuver so we can confirm it.

Jim Lovell @JLCDRApollo13
Houston needs to tell us the time to turn off the ascent oxygen in case we totally lose contact with them. We're only hearing about half of each other's words right now.

Joe Kerwin @JKerwinCAPCOM
Apollo 13 is GO to begin the right yaw maneuver. If we no longer have enough radio signal after the maneuver, they will need to bring the power amplifier back up, costing the spacecraft more power they can't afford.

Joe Kerwin @JKerwinCAPCOM
We copied the new attitude of the spacecraft. Voice from Apollo 13 is a little better now. We still have a lot of noise, but if they talk slowly I think we can manage.

Jim Lovell @JLCDRApollo13
Comms is very, very noisy on this end. This won't do at all.

Joe Kerwin @JKerwinCAPCOM
INCO is checking into what we can do about the noise. It may be a problem with the new site after we switched Earth stations.

Walter Cronkite @WCronkiteCBSNews
If all goes well, the command module of Apollo 13 (which by that point will be the re-entry vehicle) will splash down in the Pacific Ocean north of New Zealand at about 1 p.m. Eastern Standard Time on Friday.

Walter Cronkite @WCronkiteCBSNews
All the world is watching and hoping. The U.S. Senate passed a resolution today calling for all Americans to pause at 9 p.m. tonight, 45 minutes before the next burn, to pray for the safe return of the Apollo 13 astronauts.

Jules Bergman @JBABCNews
Right now, the situation seems to be under control. The world is praying and hoping for the best.

Jules Bergman @JBABCNews
The families of the astronauts are at their respective homes, and Mrs. Haise says she does not feel as tense today as she did last night.

Jules Bergman @JBABCNews
Mrs. Lovell plans a communion service in her home. Apparently, the parents of the lone bachelor on the mission, Jack Swigert, held a prayer session in their home in Denver in the very early hours of this morning.

2 days 16 hours mission time

Joe Kerwin @JKerwinCAPCOM
We are going to try to fix the comms and telemetry signals by temporarily breaking off and re-acquiring.

Jim Lovell @JLCDRApollo13
In order to save another amp or two of power, we're going to go to down voice backup configuration and pull the power amp circuit. We will start the next yaw maneuver 29 minutes from now.

Joe Kerwin @JKerwinCAPCOM
Apollo 13 is just about readable through the noise, but they say they can now hear us fine.

Fred Haise @FHLMPilotApollo13
Houston didn't understand my last request due to the voice break up. I asked them how long we have been living on the lunar module and using its power.

Jim Lovell @JLCDRApollo13
The lunar module has a fair amount of power right now, so we're looking at the possibility of powering up one of the command module's electrical buses via an umbilical connection from the lunar module.

Joe Kerwin @JKerwinCAPCOM
Communication with Apollo 13 is now back to normal. We want the crew to do an alignment procedure using the optical telescope in a little over 3 hours. This is the best chance they have of successful course correction now.

Fred Haise @FHLMPilotApollo13
As well as using the Earth-Sun alignment, Houston will give us a star to use as a check when we are in darkness. It looks like we will need a 900 foot per second maneuver to get us to a Pacific splashdown at around 142 hours.

Joe Kerwin @JKerwinCAPCOM
Freddo just told us that Jim and Jack are taking a nap in the upstairs bedroom right now. I didn't know we had an upstairs, but Freddo tells me they now have the world's first space station. Much laughter down here.

Fred Haise @FHLMPilotApollo13
I just made another yaw maneuver. I may have allowed a little too much roll.

Jim Lovell @JLCDRApollo13
This kind of navigation was not planned for while Odyssey and Aquarius are in a docked configuration, but Houston tell me that they have just run tests in the simulator using just such a docked configuration.

Charlie Duke @CDukeNASA
In the simulator, to control pitch and roll we used the thrust controller which the crew are familiar with, but to control yaw we used the ACA.

Charlie Duke @CDukeNASA
Dave Scott has been running these procedures in the simulator for a while now and we'll be able to send up detailed procedures to Apollo 13 soon.

Jim Lovell @JLCDRApollo13
I have to say I don't have a lot of confidence in this realignment of the spaceship using complex Earth-Sun readings. I don't think Houston knows how often I have screwed up on my arithmetic.

Eric Sevareid @ESCBSNews
While 3 imperiled young men circle the Moon, the accident has come at a bad time for this government. Too much has been happening in these

last 2 weeks. Too much of it adverse, painful and acrimonious.

Eric Sevareid @ESCBSNews
Everyone is thinking of the 3 men most of all, but there is the knowledge that if a tragedy occurs it will be one of the most tragic and dramatized of all time and can only deepen the spiritual miasma that already weighs upon the capital.

Eric Sevareid

Eric Sevareid was a prominent CBS news reporter and war correspondent from 1939 to 1977. He was the first to report the fall of Paris when it was captured by the Germans in 1939. In 1963, along with Walter Cronkite, he gave extensive commentary on the assassination of President John F. Kennedy, the Apollo program and the Vietnam War. Unlike many journalists, Sevareid was considered to be a reporter with 'attitude' and openly admitted to his own political biases.

Eric Sevareid @ESCBSNews
Whether the men make it back or not, there are bound to be weeks of investigation and the future of the Apollo program is bound to be affected.

Eric Sevareid @ESCBSNews
Had this accident happened during the first Moon landing attempt, efforts would probably have been redoubled. But Americans have twice walked the Moon already and the public mood has changed.

Eric Sevareid @ESCBSNews
Moon exploration still excites scientists, but not many others outside their ranks. A difficult question may be raised on a national scale: When is enough enough? Questions that have long been raised regarding nuclear weapons and the Vietnam War.

Gene Kranz @GKFlgtDirApollo13
We will power down the primary guidance system after the next burn, power up two more times for mid courses and hope to land with still about 12 or 13 hours of water and cooling available.

Walter Cronkite @WCronkiteCBSNews
There are a great deal of imponderables left. They have to get rid of the now largely-useless service module, and then of the lunar module as they approach the Earth's atmosphere on Friday.

Walter Cronkite @WCronkiteCBSNews
The jettisoning procedures of those modules are going to be tricky maneuvers themselves given the limited systems now available to the astronauts.

Walter Cronkite @WCronkiteCBSNews
There is a nuclear generator aboard the lunar module. It was to have been left on the Moon to power the scientific experiment package which was the main goal of the mission.

Walter Cronkite @WCronkiteCBSNews
Mission Control assures us however that that nuclear generator poses no threat—it will be destroyed during re-entry.

Walter Cronkite @WCronkiteCBSNews
Odyssey's protective shield will then carry the crew's re-entry vehicle through the 5,000 degrees of re-entry into the Earth's atmosphere.

Nelson Bennett @NBCBSNews
At 9.40 p.m. , the commander will feed, by computer, power into the lunar module's descent engine.

Nelson Bennett @NBCBSNews
He will burn that engine for 4 minutes and 20 seconds increasing the spacecraft's speed by some 2,700 miles per hour.

Walter Cronkite @WCronkiteCBSNews
It's not likely that any 3 men have ever waged such a dramatic battle so fully in the attention of the world.

Walter Cronkite @WCronkiteCBSNews
Foreign newspapers are saying that the concern this crisis creates is as great as the work undertaken, and results in a unique human solidarity never before seen.

Jim Lovell @JLCDRApollo13
We have the upper right corner of the Sun. It's not quite centered, a little bit less than a diameter… just to one side.

Vance Brand @VBrandCAPCOM
The flight director attitude indicator has the following attitudes for the maneuver: yaw 060 degrees, pitch 083 degrees, roll 272 degrees.

Jim Lovell @JLCDRApollo13
There's something screwed up on our burn attitude. We're not getting the proper readings. I'm not sure what is wrong. We need to go through the procedure again.

Vance Brand @VBrandCAPCOM
The spaceship's angles are looking good from down here. We can't explain Jim's attitude needle error thing, but we recommend they continue with the maneuver.

Jim Lovell @JLCDRApollo13
Our pitch and yaw needles are working their way in now because we got a 270-degree roll and our pitch and yaw needles are reversed.

Jim Lovell @JLCDRApollo13
I'm going to close my eyes for a while. Fred is taking over. There are things he needs to talk over with Charlie Duke at Mission Control.

Jim Lovell @JLCDRApollo13
Uh oh! Just had another battery alarm in the lunar module.

Fred Haise @FHLMPilotApollo13
All this navigating and making attitude adjustments by looking out of the windows at the stars means we're pretty much flying by the seat of our pants at the moment.

> **EVENING CHRONICLE**
> Oxygen-starved spacemen battle way round moon
> **CRIPPLED APOLLO IN 'LIFE OR DEATH' RACE FOR HOME**

David Brinkley @DBNBCNews
Apparently, there is some heating trouble in an electrical battery in the lunar module. There's no telling now how serious this might be since the alarm bell just rang in the spacecraft and was reported by Commander Lovell.

Walter Cronkite @WCronkiteCBSNews
The Apollo 13 spacecraft is now about a quarter of its way back from the Moon and slightly off course as it limps home tonight.

Walter Cronkite @WCronkiteCBSNews
But the spaceship's present course will not bring it back to Earth. On this course, it would miss Earth by 104 miles and the crew would perish in space.

Walter Cronkite @WCronkiteCBSNews
A critical burn (or mid-course correction as they call it) is needed to correct its course and is scheduled for 11.33 Eastern Time tonight.

Walter Cronkite @WCronkiteCBSNews
However, not everything is going as smoothly as NASA may have hoped just a few hours ago. Our correspondent, Bruce Morton, is about to update us on the latest developments.

Bruce Morton @BMCBSNews
I am reporting that the lithium hydroxide canisters which clean the air for the astronauts may not be enough to maintain breathable air for all three astronauts inside the lunar module.

Bruce Morton @BMCBSNews
The canisters inside the command module are not interchangeable with those in the lunar module. One set has round connectors, the other set has square connectors.

Bruce Morton @BMCBSNews
In addition, the astronauts are reporting that more gas is venting from the crippled service module and they are having trouble rotating the spacecraft so that heat inside the cabin is maintained at a tolerable level.

Walter Cronkite @WCronkiteCBSNews
Earlier this evening still another problem cropped up. A battery aboard the lunar module began overheating and had to be switched off. That will cut that precious margin of power available to the lunar module.

Bruce Morton @BMCBSNews
Houston continues to have sporadic problems with cutouts in communications with the astronauts.

Bruce Morton @BMCBSNews
All of these are minor problems, but are making the work of the astronauts and the support staff on the ground just that much more stressful.

David Brinkley @DBNBCNews
Late tonight, they are scheduled to make one more course correction. At about 11.45 p.m., they will twist the spacecraft around in space and aim its rocket engine at the Earth.

David Brinkley @DBNBCNews
They will fire that rocket engine for about 15 seconds which will reduce the speed of the spacecraft by a tiny fraction, about 5 mph. This will be enough to aim the spacecraft about 80 miles closer to the Earth.

David Brinkley @DBNBCNews
When the spacecraft is close to the Earth, the gravity of the Earth will start to bring down the spacecraft on Friday.

David Brinkley @DBNBCNews
On its present course without correction, the spacecraft would not be captured by the Earth's gravity and it wouldn't land.

David Brinkley @DBNBCNews
Apollo 13 is now 190,000 miles roughly from the Earth, currently travelling at 2,900 mph.

Fred Haise @FHLMPilotApollo13
So much detailed instruction coming up from Houston right now. I can hardly find time to eat due to all the navigation and spaceship attitude adjustments I'm having to do.

Wally Schirra @WSchirraNASA
Using the thrusters of the lunar module to rotate the entire configuration is not something that has been done before even in the simulator.

Wally Schirra @WSchirraNASA
We are hearing that Jim Lovell is having problems maneuvering right now because the center of mass is so different with the 3 modules attached.

Walter Cronkite @WCronkiteCBSNews
We are also hearing from NASA that they are considering jettisoning the service module (which isn't doing them any good right now) in the hope that this would alleviate the center of mass/maneuvering problem.

Wally Schirra @WSchirraNASA
However, one function the service module is performing right now is to isolate the heat shield of the re-entry vehicle (the command module Odyssey) from the extreme cold of space.

Wally Schirra @WSchirraNASA
If the heat shield was to suffer cracking or other damage due to the extreme cold of space, the re-entry of Odyssey could result in a fiery inferno of the re-entry vehicle and the total loss of the mission.

Walter Cronkite @WCronkiteCBSNews
All the modules will have to be jettisoned at some point so that the command module can return to Earth as the re-entry vehicle.

Walter Cronkite @WCronkiteCBSNews
If any of the other modules remain attached, the thermodynamics are all wrong and it just wouldn't work.

Walter Cronkite @WCronkiteCBSNews
If the lunar module or the service module were to remain attached during re-entering the Earth's atmosphere, they would burn up in the atmosphere as the heat shield at the base of the command module would not be in the correct attitude.

Wally Schirra @WSchirraNASA
Unlike on previous flights where all three crewmembers have been able to sleep simultaneously, from now on there will always be one crewmember awake in general quarters/battle stations mode.

Walter Cronkite @WCronkiteCBSNews
The situation is certainly critical and it has been called "the most serious situation we have ever faced in space."

Walter Cronkite @WCronkiteCBSNews
However, the NASA managers in their recent press conference have stated that the astronauts have a good chance of returning safely to Earth.

Vance Brand @VBrandCAPCOM
For our consumables analysis, we need to confirm that Apollo 13 is getting drinking water out of the

command module into the lunar module and have them estimate how much they will use as time goes on.

Fred Haise @FHLMPilotApollo13
Jack filled as many bags of water in the command module as he could before it freezes and brought them into Aquarius. He made up 10 bags of approximately 8 ounces per bag.

Jack Swigert @JSCMPApollo13
I just spilled a whole lot of water all over my boots. Freddo says it will dry, but it's more likely it will freeze before it can dry. I may have to sit out the journey with a pair of frozen feet.

Vance Brand @VBrandCAPCOM
Apollo 13 is now GO for this critical burn. A lot of finger crossing going on down here in Mission Control.

Vance Brand @VBrandCAPCOM
Two minutes and 40 seconds to go to burn.

Vance Brand @VBrandCAPCOM
That was incorrect. Three minutes plus. Now counting down to 3 minutes.

Vance Brand @VBrandCAPCOM
One minute.

Jim Lovell @JLCDRApollo13
Commencing burn. Now burning at 40 percent.

Jim Lovell @JLCDRApollo13
Now burning at 80%

Vance Brand @VBrandCAPCOM
The burn is looking good at 2 minutes.

Jim Lovell @JLCDRApollo13
SHUTDOWN.

Vance Brand @VBrandCAPCOM
I'd say that was a pretty good burn. A lot of relieved faces down here.

3 days 8 hours mission time

Walter Cronkite @WCronkiteCBSNews
The interesting possibility was raised at the NASA news conference that the spaceship was hit by a meteoroid.

Walter Cronkite @WCronkiteCBSNews
This has always been considered a possible danger in space, but it has been pretty well dismissed as man has ventured further out there.

Walter Cronkite @WCronkiteCBSNews
But it does seem that a large explosion took place in the service module (that is the large section behind the command module) and it caused a venting of oxygen.

Walter Cronkite @WCronkiteCBSNews
Due to power limitations and the need to conserve as much electrical power as possible, from this point onwards NASA will not power up their strongest antenna, so communications with the astronauts could be a bit spotty.

Walter Cronkite @WCronkiteCBSNews
Flight Commander Jim Lovell is reporting now that he again cannot see stars out of the lunar module windows.

Walter Cronkite @WCronkiteCBSNews
Presumably, this is because the windows are covered with debris from the explosion. So problems of alignment become much more difficult.

Wally Schirra @WSchirraNASA
They can't go out and turn on window wipers to clean the dirty windows, so I'm not sure what the crew can do about that.

Wally Schirra @WSchirraNASA
But they do need to be able to see known stars to maneuver to correct alignments for return and re-entry. That is critical.

Vance Brand @VBrandCAPCOM
The crew have an issue with the carbon dioxide build up in the lunar module. We have a team figuring out a workaround fix to scrub the air and hope to be able to send up a procedure shortly.

Vance Brand @VBrandCAPCOM
The fix will be kind of like putting a model airplane together using whatever improvised materials we can use from the spacecraft. There is a lot of out-of-the-box thinking going into this one.

Vance Brand @VBrandCAPCOM
The contraption will look something like a mailbox when it is complete, but it has to work as a perfect technological fix—we don't want to lose the crew due to lack of breathable air.

Roy Neal @RNealCBSNews
We have learned that a group of astronauts are working in a simulator here in the Manned Space Center. They are trying to duplicate the conditions the men out in space are facing right now.

Roy Neal @RNealCBSNews
Power at the moment is the critical factor aboard the lunar module. Controllers continue to work out more ways of minimizing the astronauts' use of what little electrical power remains aboard the spacecraft.

Walter Cronkite @WCronkiteCBSNews
The environmental control system in the command and service module is powered down now to conserve power, so the crew are now relying on the environmental control system of the lunar module.

Walter Cronkite @WCronkiteCBSNews
A key component of their environment is, of course, breathable air.

Wally Schirra @WSchirraNASA
To ensure sufficient filtered, breathable air, the spacecraft uses lithium hydroxide canisters in the command module.

Wally Schirra @WSchirraNASA
The air in spacecraft is circulated through these canisters and they filter out the impurities and the carbon dioxide.

Chet Huntley @CHNBC News
At the command spacecraft center today, they took one whole shift of flight controllers out of Mission

Control and set them to thinking up ways to get around the problems still ahead.

Chet Huntley @CHNBC News
One of the problems the teams are looking at is the air inside the spacecraft. They are setting up a jerry-rigged system of cleaning the air of the carbon dioxide the crew are breathing out.

Chet Huntley @CHNBC News
There are some pieces of metal, apparently blown out by the explosion, which are flying alongside the spaceship.

Chet Huntley @CHNBC News
If one of these pieces of metal should lock onto the heat shield during re-entry, it could in its burning burn a dangerous hole in the shield.

Jules Bergman @JBABCNews
The astronauts have run out of air-purifying canisters (lithium hydroxide units) in the lunar module. The canisters inside the lunar module were not meant to handle the air for two spacecraft modules.

Dick Spray @DSABCNews
The five filters in the lunar module were only meant for 2 astronauts for a day and a half.

Jules Bergman @JBABCNews
The problem with the air-purifying canisters is that those in the command module take square cartridges, whereas those in the lunar module take round cartridges.

Dick Spray @DSABCNews
The lithium hydroxide canisters from the command module are also larger than those in the lunar module, so they can't be interchanged.

Dick Spray @DSABCNews
There are 15 of the larger canisters inside the command module which is enough if they are able to improvise a way to install them in the lunar module.

Jules Bergman @JBABCNews
Space agency officials have begun investigating the explosion and now believe that it was an oxygen tank that blew up. How it happened they don't know.

Jules Bergman @JBABCNews
NASA officials don't think it was a meteor hit, but they're not sure and perhaps never will be.

Jules Bergman @JBABCNews
The astronauts will stay in the lunar module (their lifeboat) until the last possible minute before re-entry.

Jules Bergman @JBABCNews
The command module batteries only have a few hours of power left in them, and that's what has Space Agency officials really worried.

Wally Schirra @WSchirraNASA
The concern here is, with the command module powered down, whether the lithium hydroxide canisters in the lunar module can do this job sufficient to ensure breathable air for all 3 astronauts sitting in the lunar module.

Walter Cronkite @WCronkiteCBSNews
The lithium hydroxide canisters in the lunar module were only designed to ensure breathable air for 2 astronauts for a fairly short amount of time—the lunar landing. Not for 3 men for most of the length of the flight.

Walter Cronkite @WCronkiteCBSNews
There's no shortage of oxygen. The problem is power for the compressor to drive the used air through the lithium hydroxide system and having enough functionality in the remaining canisters to scrub enough air for the crew.

Wally Schirra @WSchirraNASA
The controllers and the astronauts will certainly be keeping a very close watch on the amount of carbon dioxide building up in the cabin. This could present a real problem in a very short amount of time.

Walter Cronkite @WCronkiteCBSNews
Another critical issue facing the astronauts is that of temperature inside the spacecraft. The temperature out there can be 450 plus or 450 minus depending on whether you're on the sunny or shadow side of the Sun.

Walter Cronkite @WCronkiteCBSNews
The astronauts can't stay in one position too long or they'd bake on one side and freeze on the other. So they turn the spacecraft around slowly—one revolution an hour I believe.

Wally Schirra @WSchirraNASA
In order to rotate the three attached modules of the spacecraft now they are in an improvised emergency configuration.

Wally Schirra @WSchirraNASA
They will be using the small jets at the base of the lunar module to rotate the stack. Of course, this uses up power and they don't have a lot of that right now.

Jim Lovell @JLCDRApollo13
Just prior to going around the Moon, we saw a lot of debris that was floating with us, including one rather large piece that looked like some kind of wrapping. It's still with us.

Jim Lovell @JLCDRApollo13
The thing has stayed with us, even after our last mid-course burn. I can roll the spacecraft either way but still can't shake it off.

Fred Haise @FHLMPilotApollo13
We just got a MASTER ALARM. Looks like it was tripped by the carbon dioxide level which is very high now.

Jim Lovell @JLCDRApollo13
As well as the master alarm, we now have a blinking CO_2 light. We might have to have Houston speed up this CO_2 scrubbing rig they are speaking about.

Fred Haise @FHLMPilotApollo13
I've asked Houston to tell us what sort of material they have in mind to have us build this CO_2-scrubbing 'mailbox' out of. I assume we'll use the space-age baling wire or duct tape.

Vance Brand @VBrandCAPCOM
Fred is right—comical as it sounds. They'll use plastic as a covering for the whole thing. Put some kind of stiffener at the top, and duct tape to stick the whole thing together.

Technicians at Mission Control demonstrating the improvised CO_2 scrubbing device

Vance Brand @VBrandCAPCOM
They'll need something like a sock to put in the bottom so the outlet side is plugged up. Well get back to them in a while with details as to exactly how this jerry-rigged CO_2 scrubber cartridge needs to be put together.

Jim Lovell @JLCDRApollo13
I guess I'd better eat something. This sachet has some of that candied jelly. We've gone a hell of a long time without sleep. I got hardly any sleep last night at all.

Jim Lovell @JLCDRApollo13
We're taking stock of how much water we have and thinking of rationing some of it. I'd hate to run out of water on the last day, so we're saving all the water we can.

Jim Lovell @JLCDRApollo13
The stuff that's good to eat now will be the candies, the sandwich spreads. Maybe the dehydrated stuff, but if we have to re-hydrate it, it will be kind of difficult.

Jack Swigert @JSCMPApollo13
We're told that Tony and Jack at Mission Control have been putting a big effort into figuring out how we can improvise the CO_2 scrubber cartridge from what we have on the spacecraft. Hope to have details soon.

3 days 10 hours mission time

Charlie Duke @CDukeNASA
Consumables update indicates the crew have 215 pounds of usable water available and 120 hours of oxygen remaining. But the oxygen will be no use if they are not able to scrub out the excess CO_2 from the spacecraft.

Vance Brand @VBrandCAPCOM
Deke says the crew ought to get some sleep. They've been working real hard and ought to relax a bit and be ready for tomorrow.

Jack Swigert @JSCMPApollo13
Houston accepts my evaluation that power from main bus B is good despite the explosion. They suggest we stop worrying and go to sleep.

Vance Brand @VBrandCAPCOM
Aquarius have closed the heaters to save power so the astronauts will be getting very cold from here on in. Time for Jim and Jack to get some sleep after they wake Freddo up.

Jim Lovell @JLCDRApollo13
My main concern right now is the continuing CO_2 rise in the spacecraft. Hoping Houston is getting a real good handle on that.

Jack Lousma @JLousmaCAPCOM
We're about able to send Apollo 13 the procedures for CO_2 scrubber cartridge fix. Jim Lovell says they don't want to go to sleep worrying about the continued rise in CO_2.

Bruce Morton @BMCBSNews
If it weren't so foggy here in Houston, we would be able to show all the cars heading into Mission Control—astronauts, trajectory analysts, systems engineers, everyone is coming in to try to help save this crew.

Bruce Morton @BMCBSNews
We have learned that the astronauts of the Apollo 13 backup crew, including the dropped astronaut Ken Mattingly, are still in the simulator trying to work out a whole range of alternate solutions for the astronauts in space.

Bruce Morton @BMCBSNews
NASA has talked to the people at Pratt and Whitney who make the fuel cells. They are as baffled as everyone else as to what happened in the Apollo service module.

Bruce Morton @BMCBSNews
Vice-President Agnew who was to have made a visit here tomorrow has cancelled that now. Presumably on the understanding that this is an emergency.

Bruce Morton @BMCBSNews
Everybody is working really hard here and it isn't really the day for a ceremonial kind of visit.

Bruce Morton @BMCBSNews
Mrs. Lovell, the wife of flight commander Jim Lovell, is at home with her children, all of them up, all of them listening to the air to ground conversations which NASA always pipes into the astronauts' homes.

Bruce Morton @BMCBSNews
Mrs. Fred Haise is at home too. She's had some expert advice about what's going on from two astronaut guests: Neil Armstrong and Alan Bean.

Fred Haise @FHLMPilotApollo13
When I was upstairs a minute ago, I noticed some new venting from the service module. I also saw one chunk of loose metal that was tumbling around. Looked like it had come from somewhere inside the service module.

Bruce Morton @BMCBSNews
One argument against an Atlantic landing is that the landing would be 133 hours into the flight and would be 3.a.m. at that site, making a landing in darkness where there probably won't be any ships waiting for them.

Bruce Morton @BMCBSNews
Any ships and aircraft looking for the re-entry vehicle in the Atlantic would have a hard time spotting them in the darkness.

Bruce Morton @BMCBSNews
NASA would much prefer a Pacific landing, although that would have to be some 9 hours later than an Atlantic landing.

Fred Haise @FHLMPilotApollo13
Well, the Moon is getting smaller right now, so I take that to be a good sign. I'll say this—Aquarius really has been a winner, doing something it was never designed to do and keeping us alive.

Fred Haise @FHLMPilotApollo13
Jack has just returned from the command module and reports the same thing I did. There is still something venting out into space from the service module.

Jack Swigert @JSCMPApollo13
We can't tell if this venting has been continuing since the explosion or if it is something new. Either way, we need the service module to be in reasonable shape for a while longer if we are to make it back to Earth.

Jack Lousma @JLousmaCAPCOM
We're working on some camera angles in the hope the astronauts can get in a position to send us some images of the venting or whatever else is going on outside the spacecraft.

Jack Lousma @JLousmaCAPCOM
For the moment, we're not going to bother the skipper with photography. We'll wait until he has completed his rest period.

Jack Lousma @JLousmaCAPCOM
However, Freddo is keen to get into position to use his beloved Hasselblad surface camera. That is the camera which was meant to take stills on the Moon's surface.

Jack Lousma @JLousmaCAPCOM
The CO_2 reading on the spacecraft is higher than what we are reading on the ground. We've asked the astronauts to give us a CO_2 status report every 30 minutes.

Jack Swigert @JSCMPApollo13
CO_2 reading is now below 13. Not good. Not good at all. We need to get to work on this improvised fix pretty sharpish.

Jack Lousma @JLousmaCAPCOM
On my monitor, I'm now reading that Apollo 13 is 16,214 miles from the Moon, moving at around 4,500 feet per second.

Fred Haise @FHLMPilotApollo13
From the sounds of all the work that is going on back in Houston, this flight is a lot bigger test for the systems guys on the ground than it is for us up here.

Jack Lousma @JLousmaCAPCOM
Everybody down here in Mission Control is 100% optimistic. We may be on the upside of this whole thing now.

Fred Haise @FHLMPilotApollo13
I like the optimism from Houston. We had better be in good shape, particularly ourselves, rested for that re-entry day. I think that's going to be a pretty busy one.

Jack Lousma @JLousmaCAPCOM
We're considering another mid-course correction at 104 hours—about 18 hours from now... only 7 feet per second.

Jack Lousma @JLousmaCAPCOM
There may have been a misunderstanding earlier about the drinking water. The astronauts need not worry about it and drink all they want.

Jack Lousma @JLousmaCAPCOM
The flight surgeon also recommends they use some of the fruit juices as well.

Gene Kranz @GKFlgtDirApollo13
We can't hear Freddo right now. Too much background noise. We may need to use another antenna.

Fred Haise @FHLMPilotApollo13
Just broke off from Mission Control to tear into some beef and gravy, plus other assorted goodies.

Jack Lousma @JLousmaCAPCOM
I assume Freddo is gorging on the best rations with the approval of the commander. If I were the commander, I'd make him sign out everything he eats.

Jack Lousma @JLousmaCAPCOM
I asked Freddo, when he's not chewing on all that beef, to give us a CO_2 reading. He reports it's still at 13 roughly but continuing to worsen.

Fred Haise @FHLMPilotApollo13
If this flight makes it back, we'll really be able to figure out what a lunar module like Aquarius can do.

I'd say if Aquarius had a heat shield, we should bring it home.

Fred Haise @FHLMPilotApollo13
Still seeing thousands of sparkles out of the spacecraft window. Looks like we're in the middle of the Milky Way. Several thousand little sparkles at various ranges.

Fred Haise @FHLMPilotApollo13
The sparkles are all moving. I can occasionally make out a real star from among the bunch of them, but it really does break up the capability to make out a complete star pattern we could use for navigation.

Gene Kranz @GKFlgtDirApollo13
My White Team are still scratching our heads trying to figure out what these sparkles are, what can be causing them and exactly what is venting from the service module.

3 days 12 hours mission time

Deke Slayton @DKDrctrFlghtCrwOps
We're trying to figure out who will be the most tired on Apollo 13. Freddo hasn't had any sleep since before the last burn.

Fred Haise @FHLMPilotApollo13
We should get pretty much caught up on sleep during the next two days. The Earth just went by my window at about 18 degrees.

Jack Lousma @JLousmaCAPCOM
Too much background noise right now to hear the astronauts. We'll wait 10 minutes and try again.

Jack Lousma @JLousmaCAPCOM
Okay. We're hearing Freddo a little clearer now.

Fred Haise @FHLMPilotApollo13
The Moon just went by my window again at about minus 14 degrees.

Jack Lousma @JLousmaCAPCOM
We've just received the latest data on the landing area. It should be about 560 miles south of Samoa. Waves are going to be 5 feet, winds 15 knots and visibility 20 miles.

Jack Lousma @JLousmaCAPCOM
Looks like Apollo 13 is about 15 on the CO_2 level. Comms are bad again. I can hear someone speaking behind the background noise but can't make out what they're saying.

Jim Lovell @JLCDRApollo13
I've just relieved Freddo and am now back in command. I got up earlier than anticipated—it's freezing back in the command module. Not at all conducive to a good night's sleep.

Jack Lousma @JLousmaCAPCOM
Communications with the spacecraft are down again. This is not good and getting very frustrating.

Jack Lousma @JLousmaCAPCOM
Incredibly busy at Mission Control right now. We have a group working on the next mid course correction, attitudes and alignment.

Jack Lousma @JLousmaCAPCOM
Also a group working on the re-entry and how to power up the command and service modules, and

another group ready to give us the precise details of the improvised CO_2 scrubber.

Jack Lousma @JLousmaCAPCOM
I can hear Jim Lovell talking now, but can't make out what he's saying. We are tracking them at 22,500 miles out from the Moon, moving at 4,400 feet per second.

Jim Lovell @JLCDRApollo13
I'm figuring out what we should leave behind in Aquarius once we separate and ditch our 'lifeboat'. I'm thinking the spacesuits and camera equipment as well as a lot of smaller items.

Jack Lousma @JLousmaCAPCOM
We're still trying to get communications back to a level at which we can make out what the crew are saying. About to do another voice check.

Gene Kranz @GKFlgtDirApollo13
When we get back in communication, we need to have the crew rapidly construct one of the improvised lithium hydroxide rigs in the hope of scrubbing out the CO_2 which continues to increase.

Jack Lousma @JLousmaCAPCOM
We're looking at having the crew do a 7-foot-per-second midcourse correction at 104 hours. We'll send up the procedures when we are able to establish reasonable comms.

Dan Rather @DRCBSNews
This most harrowing of man's adventures in space has gripped all Americans including The President of the United States.

Dan Rather @DRCBSNews
The President today drove through heavy rain to the Goddard Space Flight Center outside Washington for an extensive briefing on the drama in space.

Dan Rather @DRCBSNews
Former astronaut Michael Collins and senior Goddard facility technicians accompanied the President and all answered his many questions about the present condition of the astronauts and their spacecraft.

Dan Rather @DRCBSNews
Earlier, the President had spoken twice by telephone to Dr. Thomas Payne, the head of the Space Agency in Houston.

Jim Lovell @JLCDRApollo13
Looks like Houston have fixed the comms. They're coming through much clearer now. Hope it's not just a temporary fix.

Dan Rather @DRCBSNews
The President was told immediately last night of the emergency aboard Apollo 13. He stayed up until after midnight getting reports and was awakened at 3 a.m. for updated information.

Dan Rather @DRCBSNews
During today, the President will receive regular updates from NASA. He praised the astronauts' grace under pressure and the operation of the entire NASA space team under immense stress.

Gene Kranz @GKFlgtDirApollo13
The burn for the next midcourse correction has to be entirely manual. The attitude will be controlled

manually, and the start/stop on the engine will also be manual.

Dan Rather @DRCBSNews
The President is going ahead with a White House dinner tonight for the visiting Prime Minister of Denmark

Dan Rather @DRCBSNews
However, a piano recital following the dinner in the White House has been cancelled so the President can monitor tonight's spacecraft rocket firing.

Dan Rather @DRCBSNews
Whether the President goes ahead with his scheduled Vietnam report to the nation on Thursday depends on how, when and if the astronauts return.

Jack Lousma @JLousmaCAPCOM
Re-entry is going to be around the dark side of the Earth. Since they will be coming in shallow, we're going to have them burn towards the Sun to make it steeper.

Jim Lovell @JLCDRApollo13
The burns will be perpendicular to our flight path and to the Sun, giving a steeper entry angle. If our entry is too shallow, we will just bounce off the atmosphere and into space.

Jack Lousma @JLousmaCAPCOM
The burns will probably be less than a minute with cut-offs based on time. In the event of loss of communications, the crew need to have the detailed procedures in hand before they start the burns.

Jim Lovell @JLCDRApollo13
This venting that's going on is very disturbing. There's no way to know what it will do to our trajectory. It's been going on for some considerable time now. Hope Houston can figure it out.

Jack Lousma @JLousmaCAPCOM
Just passed up to the crew the latest news items from Earth. President Nixon has chosen a judge from Minnesota for the Supreme Court, and a bill giving a 6% rise to federal employees has passed the House.

Jack Lousma @JLousmaCAPCOM
The pay increase includes the President and the military. Also, the air traffic controllers have returned to work.

Jim Lovell @JLCDRApollo13
Well it's a wonderful thing that the flight controllers at Mission Control have not been on strike these past couple of days. I wonder if that federal pay increase applies to astronauts… guess it does.

Gene Kranz @GKFlgtDirApollo13
One course of action we're considering is to omit the midcourse correction burn altogether and make a total midcourse correction at say, 8 hours before reentry.

Jim Lovell @JLCDRApollo13
The venting from the service module now seems to be coming from more than one spot. It could be coming from hydrogen tanks that have become over-pressurized.

Jack Lousma @JLousmaCAPCOM
When we power up the command module tomorrow, we'll have a better idea of what this venting is and whether or not it poses a threat to the craft's approach to reentry.

3 days 17 hours mission time

Jim Lovell @JLCDRApollo13
We've set up regular watch and sleep periods here. Freddo was up for a long time, so I got up early to relieve him.

Jim Lovell @JLCDRApollo13
Jack and Freddo are now asleep, so I'm going to let them sleep as long as they can. Then we'll have an eat period and I'll turn in.

Jack Lousma @JLousmaCAPCOM
The crew are off the planned sleep/work/eat schedule we had sent up. Jim doesn't need to work that out himself. We'd prefer to do it down here and just have the crew follow it.

Jim Lovell @JLCDRApollo13
Just got a bit of a reprimand from Houston for diverting from the schedule. As soon as Jack gets up, we'll have a go at rigging up these improvised lithium hydroxide canisters... it's going to need several sets of hands.

Joe Kerwin @JKerwinCAPCOM
The equipment the crew need to gather includes: two lithium hydroxide canisters, a roll of duct tape, and 2 plastic bags.

Joe Kerwin @JKerwinCAPCOM
Also, one cardboard cue card from the lunar module from which they'll need to cut off about an inch and a half out from the ring.

Jack Swigert @JSCMPApollo13
Hey! Just heard that I got a 6-day extension on my income tax due to being out of the country. I think halfway between the Moon and the Earth qualifies as 'out of the country'.

Jim Lovell @JLCDRApollo13
Jack's up now. As soon as he gets on his helmet, he'll be ready to copy and start making one of these jerry-rigged and experimental lithium hydroxide CO_2 scrubbing devices.

Jack Swigert @JSCMPApollo13
Now starting to rig up this space-age plastic and cardboard life-saving CO_2 scrubbing contraption. They've tested it down at Mission Control, so here's hoping.

Joe Kerwin @JKerwinCAPCOM
Relaying detailed instructions on building the CO_2 scrubber, but the really bad comms signal is not helping. We're just hoping Jack is receiving us reasonably clearly and is following the procedure to the letter.

Jack Swigert @JSCMPApollo13
Goddamn! This is a really involved finicky procedure. So many instructions from Houston, but I think I'm following them correctly. The thing is definitely coming together.

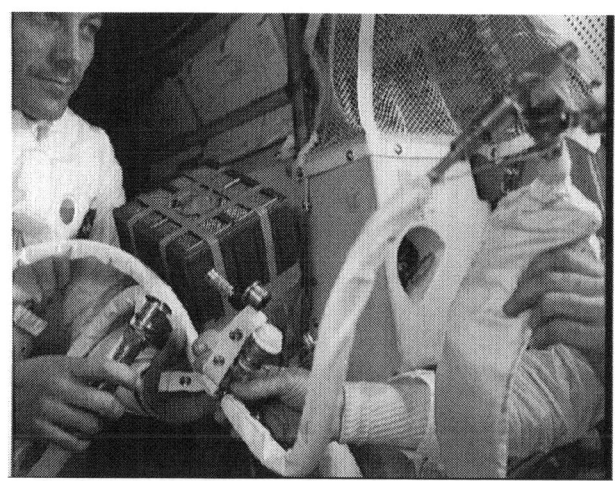

Jack Swigert with the CO_2 srubbing 'mailbox'

Jack Swigert @JSCMPApollo13
Well, it took the best part of an hour but I think I've got it done. NASA's first CO_2 scrubber connector built entirely with plastic bags, cardboard, duct tape and NASA rapid-fire ingenuity.

Jim Lovell @JLCDRApollo13
Jack is now connecting the improvised CO_2 scrubber and mounting it out of our way. Strange to have your life dependent on a hastily-rigged cardboard box contraption held together with duct tape.

Jack Swigert @JSCMPApollo13
Don't know yet if the thing will work, but it looks surprisingly functional. And built for the low, low price of $3.99. Hope Houston have sent in a patent application for the device.

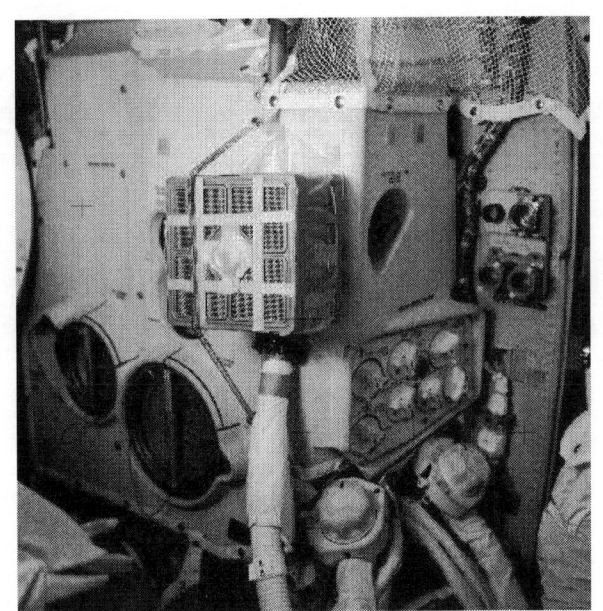

The completed CO_2 scrubbing device mounted inside the lunar module

3 days 20 hours mission time

Joe Kerwin @JKerwinCAPCOM
The next order of business is to ensure that the electrical power from MAIN BUS B is good. If it is, we'll read up a procedure for transferring the lunar module power to the command module.

Jack Swigert @JSCMPApollo13
We're all sitting here having a food break, but Joe just told me that Deke is strongly insisting that Jim go back to bed. I'll get the switch configuration done now so I won't disturb Jim while he's sleeping.

Jack Swigert @JSCMPApollo13
Jim says Deke sounds like Frank Bormann on Apollo 8. Much merriment at that up here.

Fred Haise @FHLMPilotApollo13
I'm back on comms now having logged 6 hours sleep. It's really chilly in here. We made the mistake of putting up the window shades which we won't do again. We need all the internal heat we can get.

Fred Haise @FHLMPilotApollo13
We haven't had an overboard waste water dump since back around the other side of the Moon. We're running out of the urine bags we've got on board here.

Jim Lovell @JLCDRApollo13
Oh boy! We have an apparent short-circuit in the lunar module electrical system accompanied by a loud thump in the vicinity of the descent stage.

Jim Lovell @JLCDRApollo13
We are seeing venting now in the area of lunar module batteries #1 and #2. Waiting to hear what Houston make of this new and unwanted development.

Walter Cronkite @WCronkiteCBSNews
The families of the astronauts remain largely in seclusion, but in Denver the father of replacement command module pilot, Jack Swigert, spoke with newsmen today.

Dr Leonard Swigert @LSwigertDenver
I sat up most of last night with my wife trying to figure out what was happening on the spaceship.

Dr Leonard Swigert @LSwigertDenver
Knowing that they now seem to have enough oxygen certainly takes a load off my mind. I'm hoping that the electrical supply will hold out.

Dr Leonard Swigert @LSwigertDenver
I just have to rely on my faith and knowledge. NASA's pretty good and I know they won't leave any stone unturned to bring those boys home.

Dr Leonard Swigert @LSwigertDenver
My wife, Jack's mother, is more emotional than I am and cracking up with worry somewhat. But like I am, she's confident that the Lord will bring us through this.

Walter Cronkite @WCronkiteCBSNews
There has been very little opportunity for the wives of the astronauts to be alone on this difficult day. There has been a great deal of coming and going at the home of astronaut Jim Lovell near the Space Center.

Walter Cronkite @WCronkiteCBSNews
The Lovell family minister visited the Lovell home this morning and conducted communion services. Mrs. Lovell remained inside her home all day, but she did send the children to school.

Walter Cronkite @WCronkiteCBSNews
At the home of astronaut Fred Haise, one of the first visitors today was Apollo 12 astronaut Alan Bean. He spent part of the morning with Mrs. Haise and the children assuring them Apollo 13's problems had stabilized.

Jim Lovell @JLCDRApollo13
Reading the CO_2 levels right now and it seems like this hastily-improvised fix might actually be working.

Alan Bean

Alan Bean joined the NASA astronaut team in 1963 as part of Astronaut Group 3. As lunar module pilot and one of the three-man crew of Apollo 12, he became the fourth man to walk on the Moon. He also flew on the Skylab 3 mission in 1973, shortly after which he retired to become a full-time painter, particularly producing works of space-related themes.

Alan Bean @ABeanApollo12
I spent some time talking with the three Haise children. They had some questions that were actually pretty technical. Kids nowadays are pretty technically-minded.

Alan Bean @ABeanApollo12
I explained to Freddo's kids where the oxygen was coming from, where they were getting the water and what had happened to some of the things that

they've been concerned about. I think they're pretty happy now.

Gene Kranz @GKFlgtDirApollo13
The crew seem to have solved any problem there was with the lunar module descent batteries. They read fine on our panels down here.

Gene Kranz @GKFlgtDirApollo13
The next thing is for the crew to go back into the command module and temporarily power up the main electrical buses to verify that there are no excess loads.

Gene Kranz @GKFlgtDirApollo13
We need the main bus tie switches in the ON position to ensure they have power whether the batteries get cold or not.

Fred Haise @FHLMPilotApollo13
I just asked Houston to see how they're reading our CO_2 levels right now. They reported CO_2 level at only 0.2 and that they're all pretty delighted. Seems like the damn contraption works... really well!

Joe Kerwin @JKerwinCAPCOM
Apollo 13 is now 40,000 miles out from the Moon, edging nearer to the Earth every minute. Comms are getting real bad again. We've told the crew again that they have to talk real loud and real slow.

Fred Haise @FHLMPilotApollo13
I'm noticing some fresh new particles drifting outside the spacecraft. I think the service module is venting out again.

Jack Swigert @JSCMPApollo13
I'm ready to copy the procedure for powering up the command module by transferring the power from the lunar module. Odyssey sure needs that... it's freezing in there.

Joe Kerwin @JKerwinCAPCOM
We're not certain when is the best time to begin the powering up procedure. But we'll read up the procedure details so they will be ready and able to do it quickly when the time comes.

Fred Haise @FHLMPilotApollo13
While Jack was on comms, I was looking out of the docking window and saw another good shower of particles coming from the service module.

Fred Haise @FHLMPilotApollo13
The position of those venting particles seems to be on the other side now—before, we'd always seen them out of window 1.

Jack Swigert @JSCMPApollo13
Houston have just sent up the procedures for powering up the command module. A whole heap of details. Now we just have to wait until it's time to implement the procedures.

Fred Haise @FHLMPilotApollo13
Jack is going upstairs to see what the venting looks like from up there.

Gene Kranz @GKFlgtDirApollo13
When Odyssey separates from the service module, we need the crew to get some pictures to see if we can access the damage caused by the explosion and try to figure out what caused it.

Fred Haise @FHLMPilotApollo13
Well, we might as well use the remaining film on the service module. We sure as hell no longer need it for its intended purpose—documenting our landing and walks on the Moon.

Fred Haise @FHLMPilotApollo13
The spacecraft's wobble is getting worse. The Earth is nearly up to the top of the window. Conversely, the Moon is way down at the bottom of the window. This is far more wobble than we had on my previous watch.

Fred Haise @FHLMPilotApollo13
We've got another powerful burst of particles going on outside the service module. Jack thinks it may be coming from the hydrogen tanks now.

Joe Kerwin @JKerwinCAPCOM
We've just had the latest report on the current state of consumables on the spacecraft. They're holding at 11 to 12 amps per hour real steady. Looks okay.

Joe Kerwin @JKerwinCAPCOM
FIDO has just informed me the spacecraft has now crossed into Earth's sphere of influence and is starting to speed up.

Jack Swigert @JSCMPApollo13
We're on our way back home.

Fred Haise @FHLMPilotApollo13
Following the detailed power up procedures, I asked Houston to send me up a procedure for separating four gingerbread cubes. I think they were stuck together with epoxy glue.

Vance Brand @VBrandCAPCOM
The gingerbread cubes were stuck together that way so they could stand the pressures of launch and booster separation.

Vance Brand @VBrandCAPCOM
Gene Kranz says Fred can use the dikes to separate the gingerbread cubes. I've sent up a detailed checklist for the procedure.

Fred Haise @FHLMPilotApollo13
I generally don't use the subtle approaches when dealing with food. I told Vance he should be able to tell we're feeling pretty good when we're complaining about gingerbread procedures.

Vance Brand @VBrandCAPCOM
People are feeling much better down here, too. And our comm signal is much better now, so we should be able to deal effectively with any further cookie issues that might arise.

100 hours mission time

Jim Lovell @JLCDRApollo13
Just had 4 or 5 hours sleep. Looks like the venting from the service module has ceased, at least momentarily. Still no idea what it was but whatever was spewing out there, we can't have much of it left on the spacecraft.

Charlie Duke @CDukeNASA
The main thing we're thinking about at Mission Control right now are the procedures for transferring control from Aquarius to the command module and the jettisoning of Aquarius.

Jim Lovell @JLCDRApollo13
We just had a battery warning MASTER ALARM, and it looks like it's battery number 2.

Charlie Duke @CDukeNASA
Jim is turning off battery number 2. He needs to leave it off so we can take a look at it.

Charlie Duke @CDukeNASA
We have determined that the battery problem is not overcurrent or reverse current. We suspect it's over-temp but we're not sure, so we're going to watch it for a while.

Charlie Duke @CDukeNASA
The upcoming midcourse correction burn will be at 105 mission hours. In establishing the correct attitude for the burn, the crew will need to damp the rates with the Earth in the forward window.

Charlie Duke @CDukeNASA
They need to get in a posture when they see the Earth come through the window, damp her out and try to hold the Earth in the window.

Jim Lovell @JLCDRApollo13
I figure I have a handle on how the Earth should appear during the midcourse correction procedure. I need some guidance from Houston as to how the Sun should look.

Charlie Duke @CDukeNASA
We'll send Jim some detail as to how the Sun should appear in his window during the burn shortly.

Charlie Duke @CDukeNASA
The shutdown of the burn should be burn time minus 1 second, e.g. if the burn is 30 seconds, shutdown should be at 29 seconds.

Charlie Duke @CDukeNASA
We need to make sure we get an exact burn time. We can't afford to risk an overburn at this point, so it's crucial to shut down at burn time minus 1 second.

Charlie Duke @CDukeNASA
During the burn, the crew will be controlling pitch and roll via the error needles. We've been practicing this in the simulator and it seems to work quite well… for the most part.

Walter Cronkite @WCronkiteCBSNews
Many nations have offered to help in the recovery of Apollo 13. Britain has sent 6 navy ships to a possible landing site in the Indian Ocean.

Walter Cronkite @WCronkiteCBSNews
France, the Netherlands, Italy, Spain, Russia, Germany, South Africa, Brazil and Uruguay have all put their navies on alert to give any possible assistance to the recovery of Apollo 13.

Walter Cronkite @WCronkiteCBSNews
The entire world is following the hazardous return of Apollo 13. Ten thousand people joined Pope John Paul in prayers for Apollo 13 in St. Peter's Basilica today.

Walter Cronkite @WCronkiteCBSNews
Special prayers for the safe return of the astronauts are also being said at the Wailing Wall in Jerusalem.

Chet Huntley @CHNBC News
The Apollo 13 astronauts are travelling back to Earth today at a speed of more than 3,200 mph. They have had to overcome all sorts of difficulties by improvising, which so far they have been able to do.

Chet Huntley @CHNBC News
Not only must the astronauts get back to Earth, but they must enter the Earth's atmosphere at the correct angle.

Chet Huntley @CHNBC News
If they are too steep by more than a degree, the spacecraft will be crushed by the Earth's atmosphere.

Chet Huntley @CHNBC News
If the spacecraft enters the atmosphere at too shallow an angle by more than a degree, 80 miles up, they will bounce off the atmosphere back into space and not be recoverable.

Chet Huntley @CHNBC News
If that happens, the crew will die in space.

Jim Lovell @JLCDRApollo13
Houston is telling me the burn time will be 15 seconds and 7.8 feet per second. This is going to be a pretty hair-raising maneuver!

Charlie Duke @CDukeNASA
Handing over capsule communications to Vance now.

Vance Brand @VBrandCAPCOM
We think the number 2 battery problem is probably a sensor failure—a temperature sensor failure that

caused the MASTER ALARM. We expect to put the battery back on at about 101 hours flight time.

Jim Lovell @JLCDRApollo13
Venting has stopped so we can now differentiate between stars and vented particles. Jack and I can now see certain constellations clearly.

Jim Lovell @JLCDRApollo13
We can see Scorpio and Sagittarius. Also large-magnitude stars like Alpha Centuri and Vega.

Jim Lovell @JLCDRApollo13
Battery number 2 is now online again, but we have a MASTER ALARM and flashing light.

Vance Brand @VBrandCAPCOM
We are convinced the battery alarm is a sensor failure and have advised the crew not to worry about it. We believe the battery is good despite the alarm.

Jim Lovell @JLCDRApollo13
We are now disconnected from any battery alarm indicators, so if there is any problem, we will not get an indication inside the spacecraft. Instead, Houston will monitor the batteries from their end.

Jack Swigert @JSCMPApollo13
Really cold inside Aquarius right now—we can see our breath. Getting ready to copy down another lengthy procedure for powering up the command and service module. Houston say 2 or 3 pages of complex detail.

Jack Swigert @JSCMPApollo13
I had to ask Vance to slow down and give me a few minutes' break. The power up procedure Houston is

sending up is a hell of a lot to note down and get it all accurately. Also getting a lot of static on the comms.

Charlie Duke @CDukeNASA
They need to power up the command and service module independent of the lunar module so we can look at the telemetry and see how cold the vehicle is—that kind of thing.

Jack Swigert @JSCMPApollo13
While I am 'upstairs' powering up the command module, I will be out of touch with Houston. Any communication will have to be through someone 'downstairs' in Aquarius.

Jack Swigert @JSCMPApollo13
Any problem and Houston will notify them and they will then dash upstairs to tell me to stop what I am doing wrong.

Jim Lovell @JLCDRApollo13
We're switching watches now and Jack is going into the command module to begin the powering up procedures. Any modifications from Houston will need to pass through me while Jack is out of comms.

Jim Lovell @JLCDRApollo13
Uh, oh! Just noticed through the overhead docking window that we are venting something out into space again.

Vance Brand @VBrandCAPCOM
We still have no answer as to what is venting from the command module. Meanwhile, we have told Jim to climb up into the 'bedroom' to tell Jack to power

down the command module once he gets his onboard readouts.

Vance Brand @VBrandCAPCOM
Telemetry from command module Odyssey indicates it's not too cold. Looks pretty good.

Jack Swigert @JSCMPApollo13
It felt real cold in Odyssey to me. I don't know if we'll be able to sleep up there tonight. It must be 35 or 40 degrees. It's not too uncomfortable in Aquarius, but it definitely is cold in Odyssey.

Jim Lovell @JLCDRApollo13
Houston is reading temperatures in Aquarius and Odyssey as being roughly the same. But we're two people in Aquarius most of the time and it seems to be a lot more compact so maybe we don't notice the cold as much.

Vance Brand @VBrandCAPCOM
We're setting up the burn for 105 hours 30 minutes mission time and are working out final procedures based on that time.

Vance Brand @VBrandCAPCOM
We noticed a 2 pound drop in the water quantity on Aquarius. Then rate went back to the previous reading. Seems like several of the craft's sensors have been playing up recently.

Vance Brand @VBrandCAPCOM
We'll have the final burn attitude adjustment procedures uploaded to Aquarius in about 15 minutes.

Vance Brand @VBrandCAPCOM
35 minutes to the burn. Aquarius will be reading 36 due to the time delay. They're maneuvering around right now, fishing for the Earth in their window.

Jack Swigert @JSCMPApollo13
Okay, we have our attitude set now. I hope the guys in the back room who thought this up knew what they were figuring.

Fred Haise @FHLMPilotApollo13
Looking through the window and the Sun's right in the top, maybe 2 degrees to the right of the cursor. Looks real good.

Vance Brand @VBrandCAPCOM
Two minutes to the burn.

Fred Haise @FHLMPilotApollo13
One minute… engine arm to descent.

Jim Lovell @JLCDRApollo13
Burning at 20%…

Jim Lovell @JLCDRApollo13
40%… 60%…

Jim Lovell @JLCDRApollo13
Burn completed. I think I've got pitch and roll squared away. Yaw is drifting in a clockwise direction.

Gene Kranz @GKFlgtDirApollo13
The burn looked good. Real good! Those guys did a fine job. One for the history books.

106 hours mission time

Jim Lovell @JLCDRApollo13
Something is flitting out there in the breeze. Seems like we're venting again. I've asked Jack to take a look.

Vance Brand @VBrandCAPCOM
Apollo 13 is now at 150,000 miles from Earth and coming in at 4,500 feet per second.

Gene Kranz @GKFlgtDirApollo13
Jack and Fred ought to get some sleep now. They need to eat in about 6 hours and the skipper ought to go to bed at about 113 hours.

Gene Kranz @GKFlgtDirApollo13
We should have some good dope on the spacecraft's trajectory in about 2 hours. Looked to us that the burn was real good, but we're taking a good look at it.

Gene Kranz @GKFlgtDirApollo13
Consumables on Apollo 13, including water, look good through at least 154 hours so we're good on that.

Jack Lousma @JLousmaCAPCOM
We're getting too much background noise to hear the crew right now. We're having to wait until they come up on a new antenna.

Jack Swigert @JSCMPApollo13
We're no longer able to get a good reading from the stars—too much visual interference from whatever is venting out of the command module.

Jack Swigert @JSCMPApollo13
We're still getting a lot of wobble on the spacecraft. It seems to be worse when there is venting from the service module.

Jack Swigert @JSCMPApollo13
We've got a MASTER ALARM. And a battery light flickering on battery 2 again. I thought we'd disconnected the battery alarms.

Jack Lousma @JLousmaCAPCOM
Voltages and currents look normal on battery 2 from down here. The crew should just ignore the alarm and battery light.

Gene Kranz @GKFlgtDirApollo13
The antenna switch is kind of annoying. If it gets too troublesome for the crew to switch antennas, they can just leave it on one antenna and we'll listen to them half of the time.

Jim Lovell @JLCDRApollo13
Fred and Jack are both going to sleep. It's sort of humorous, Fred's sleeping place now is in the tunnel, upside down with his head resting on the ascent engine.

Jim Lovell @JLCDRApollo13
Jack is on the floor of the lunar module with a restraint wrapped around his arm to keep him tied down there.

David Brinkley @DBNBCNews
Since the Apollo 13 astronauts did not land on the Moon, there will not be the usual quarantine for period after they splash down.

David Brinkley @DBNBCNews
Plans call for the three men to be flown by helicopter to Samoa, stay overnight there and then be flown directly to Houston on Saturday.

David Brinkley @DBNBCNews
The burnt out stage of the Saturn V rocket did reach the Moon. It crashed last night with great force causing a moonquake.

David Brinkley @DBNBCNews
The shake, several minutes long, registered on the seismometer that had been left on the Moon by Apollo 12 last November.

Gene Kranz @GKFlgtDirApollo13
We're planning the last midcourse correction burn at 5 hours before re-entry. We will jettison the service module at four and a half hours before re-entry.

Gene Kranz @GKFlgtDirApollo13
We'll have the crew spend the next couple of hours taking pictures of the service module to try and ascertain the damage caused by the explosion so we can get some idea what caused it.

Gene Kranz @GKFlgtDirApollo13
We'll hang onto Aquarius until 1 hour before reentry and then jettison it.

Gene Kranz @GKFlgtDirApollo13
This time, we want the crew to suit up before they jettison the lunar module so they don't have to depend solely on the hatch seal to protect them.

Jim Lovell @JLCDRApollo13
Being suited up before we jettison Aquarius would greatly impede our progress back and forth as we move between Odyssey and Aquarius.

Jim Lovell @JLCDRApollo13
But as cold as it is now, we'll probably be getting into our suits long before reentry.

Jack Lousma @JLousmaCAPCOM
Getting a huge amount of background noise now. Unless the crew are shouting, it's impossible to make out what they are saying.

Jack Lousma @JLousmaCAPCOM
How the crew will align the spacecraft for reentry while the lunar module is still attached to the back is something that's getting a lot of attention down here.

Jack Lousma @JLousmaCAPCOM
The lunar module was meant to be left behind on the Moon long before this point.

Jim Lovell @JLCDRApollo13
To line up for reentry, we will probably have to point the lunar module at the Earth and point the command module at the Moon.

Jim Lovell @JLCDRApollo13
Then we'll need to wait for Houston to align us using the Moon, the Earth or the stars.

Jim Lovell @JLCDRApollo13
Uh,oh. Another MASTER ALARM. The number 2 battery still has a light on it.

Jack Lousma @JLousmaCAPCOM
The temperature sensor on battery 2 is kind of cycling back and forth. Every time it does so, it triggers a MASTER ALARM. Same old problem. Most likely nothing to worry about, just a faulty sensor.

4 days 17 hours mission time

Jack Lousma @JLousmaCAPCOM
The reason we're asking the crew to suit up before reentry is that we can't confirm the security of the re-entry vehicle hatch.

Jack Lousma @JLousmaCAPCOM
On previous missions, we were able to confirm hatch security during lunar orbit after the command module jettisoned the lunar module. The accident ruled that out this time.

Jim Lovell @JLCDRApollo13
If the hatch fails due to the heat and trauma of reentering Earth's atmosphere, I don't see our suits giving us any protection from the inferno surrounding the reentry vehicle.

Fred Haise @FHLMPilotApollo13
We've completed the powerup procedures to transfer power back to the command module and things look good upstairs. We are now GO for proceeding with the battery charge.

Gene Kranz @GKFlgtDirApollo13
Apollo 13 is now 134,000 miles out from the Earth, coming in at 4,900 feet per second.

Fred Haise @FHLMPilotApollo13
The voltage upstairs is now 34.3, and the charger is reading 2.5 amps. Jim and Jack came back downstairs rubbing their hands. It's still really cold up there.

Fred Haise @FHLMPilotApollo13
It's still reasonably comfortable here in the lunar module. Jim and Jack have reported that the service module seems to have stopped venting.

Jack Lousma @JLousmaCAPCOM
We're barely able to hear Freddo right now—there's an awful lot of background noise.

Fred Haise @FHLMPilotApollo13
It's amazing how proficient we have become at moving through the tunnel between Aquarius and Odyssey. Of course, it helps to have done it 1,000 times now.

Gene Kranz @GKFlgtDirApollo13
The crew have to wait until there is no Sun reflection off the lunar module in order to be able to get their bearings off the stars.

Gene Kranz @GKFlgtDirApollo13
The weather prediction in the landing area is still good. 4-foot seas, 15-knot winds. There's a hurricane 500 miles to the west, but that doesn't pose a problem.

Fred Haise @FHLMPilotApollo13
Power reading now is 37.8 volts and 2.3 amps. Looks good, especially since nothing like this procedure has ever been tested before.

Gene Kranz @GKFlgtDirApollo13
The next few hours are going to be pretty quiet. We're working on the procedures for the re-entry and should be ready to send them up to Apollo 13 in about 8 hours. Meanwhile, the crew should catch up on their sleep schedule.

Joe Kerwin @JKerwinCAPCOM
Apollo 13 is now 130,000 miles out from the Earth, which is about 10,000 miles closer than when I came on a couple of hours ago. FIDO is warning they may be getting a ticket for doing 5,040 in a 5,000 mile zone.

Gene Kranz @GKFlgtDirApollo13
We have now verified that the communications problems are ground problems.

Jim Lovell @JLCDRApollo13
I'm back in command and have just heard from Houston that we are now 125,000 miles out, starting to really pick up speed as we come more and more under the Earth's influence.

Jim Lovell @JLCDRApollo13
... and that the Astros won last night.

Deke Slayton @DKDrctrFlghtCrwOps
Less than 24 hours to go to re-entry now.

Jim Lovell @JLCDRApollo13
Still really cold in Odyssey right now, but I just informed Houston that the lunar boots we had expected to be walking on the Moon in make great foot warmers. The two pairs of underwear help too.

Jim Lovell @JLCDRApollo13
Voltage is now up to 39.3, amps 1.6.

Jim Lovell @JLCDRApollo13
For future missions, the crew systems people may not need to put a refrigerator on board. I just took out a couple of hot dogs and they're practically frozen solid.

Deke Slayton @DKDrctrFlghtCrwOps
The crew are reluctant to have to climb into their suits in preparation for reentry. It's up to them, but we do a hatch integrity check one hour before reentry.

Gene Kranz @GKFlgtDirApollo13
If the hatch is busted, they'll have a real hard time scrambling into their suits in time.

Gene Kranz @GKFlgtDirApollo13
Getting into and moving in their suits would slow them down considerably. Additionally, they may get too warm and we'd have to use power to ventilate the suits—power that we can't afford.

Jim Lovell @JLCDRApollo13
The integrity check on the hatch will likely show only a slight increase in leak rate. I have confidence in the hatch as long as it goes in and locks in smoothly and solidly.

Jim Lovell @JLCDRApollo13
I see no reason to wear the suits, and one thing we are going to do in our spare time is to practice putting that hatch on to make sure we can get it on and locked.

Joe Kerwin @JKerwinCAPCOM
The jettisoning of the service module will be a very slow procedure, half a foot per second.

Joe Kerwin @JKerwinCAPCOM
The jettisoning will be slow enough that the crew should be able to get some pretty good photos that might give us an indication as to the cause of the explosion and continued venting.

Jim Lovell @JLCDRApollo13
When we are in the correct attitude to jettison the service module, I will scramble up, close the lunar module hatch and jettison it with the tunnel pressurized.

Jim Lovell @JLCDRApollo13
I just hope Jack doesn't close the hatch before I get up there.

5 days 1 hour mission time

Jim Lovell @JLCDRApollo13
After we jettison the service module, I'd like to get into a position to jettison the lunar module early and sit there for one hour before we jettison Aquarius.

Gene Kranz @GKFlgtDirApollo13
Getting to the attitude to jettison lunar module Aquarius early is permissible as soon as they have a powered up command module and a satisfactory platform.

Jim Lovell @JLCDRApollo13
Houston is telling me that the midcourse correction burn will put us right in the middle of the optimum corridor for reentry. That's good to know.

Jim Lovell @JLCDRApollo13
Latest battery readings are volts 39.5, amps 1.25.

Gene Kranz @GKFlgtDirApollo13
Looks like the crew have removed all their biomed sensors since we're not getting any readings down here. Can't say I blame them. Must be damned uncomfortable up there right now.

Vance Brand @VBrandCAPCOM
We now have Apollo 13 at 101,000 miles out from Earth and continuing to increase speed.

Fred Haise @FHLMPilotApollo13
Spent the last few hours doing stowage procedures prior to separating from the command module and then the lunar module.

Fred Haise @FHLMPilotApollo13
You wouldn't believe the lunar module right now; it's nothing but bags from floor to ceiling.

Fred Haise @FHLMPilotApollo13
Jack has just reported that he's completed and secured the battery charge now. Aquarius is back on.

Jack Swigert @JSCMPApollo13
Going back up into the 'refrigerator' now for more power up procedures for the command module. We've changed its name from 'bedroom' since it feels about 30 degrees colder up there.

Vance Brand @VBrandCAPCOM
Down here, we're reading the current temperature in the command module at 45 to 46 degrees.

Fred Haise @FHLMPilotApollo13
Any photography and sextant bearings on stars we're doing now is out of the lunar module windows.

Fred Haise @FHLMPilotApollo13
Every window in the command module is covered in droplets. It's going to take a lot of continued scrubbing to get those cleared off.

Jack Swigert @JSCMPApollo13
Battery reading now is 39.4 volts and current has jumped up to 1.4 amps. We will be charging battery A until about 126 hours 30 minutes flight time. It should be fully-charged then.

Gene Kranz @GKFlgtDirApollo13
Pretty soon, all the batteries should be up to about 116 amp-hours. That's a lot better than 99 hours. That wouldn't have done at all.

Jack Swigert @JSCMPApollo13
Houston asked what shift Jim is on. I told them every shift is morning shift up here. That's because the Sun is always shining into the spacecraft.

Jack Swigert @JSCMPApollo13
Houston won't believe this, but Fred says the power reading now is 39.4 volts and 1.245 amps.

5 days 5 hours mission time

Jim Lovell @JLCDRApollo13
Houston is about to send up instructions about which cameras, lenses and settings we should use to photograph the damage on the service module if we are able to get into a position to see it.

Vance Brand @VBrandCAPCOM
Ken Mattingly and all the hordes of people who devised the detailed procedures for jettisoning the service module, re-aligning the spacecraft and the timing of the burn are now with us.

Vance Brand @VBrandCAPCOM
Ken and his team want to listen to us sending up the procedures. The Apollo 13 crew wouldn't believe how much these procedures have been massaged and practiced in the past few hours.

Vance Brand @VBrandCAPCOM
It took a lot of people to devise this procedure. Some of them have been testing it out in the simulator. We're holding things up in the control room so they can all listen in and answer any questions the crew might have.

Vance Brand @VBrandCAPCOM
The crew should use three cameras, two through the lunar module windows and one through number 5 window of the command module.

Gene Kranz @GKFlgtDirApollo13
Best results will be from Aquarius using the Hasslelblad camera with the 80-millimeter lens, with a fresh magazine of 3,400 black-and-white film.

Ken Mattingly

Ken Mattingly was expected to pilot the command module during the Apollo 13 mission but was removed from the crew just two days before lift-off and replaced by Jack Swigert. However, during the Mission, Mattingly played a crucial role as one of the team tasked with working out power conservation and navigation procedures in the simulator and communicating these to the crew of Apollo 13. Mattingly was later to pilot the command module of the Apollo 16 successful Moon mission.

Ken Mattingly @KMLMPilotApollo13
It may be a little hard to see the service module from the command module, but if they can see it, it'll be through window 5. They should use the 250-millimeter lens with CEX film and an aperture setting of f-8.

Jack Swigert @JSCMPApollo13
It's so cold here. Temperature is around 50 in the lunar module and maybe 45 or a bit less in the command module. Houston just asked us if we're chopping up wood to keep warm.

Jack Swigert @JSCMPApollo13
All the windows in the command module are heavily coated with water right now, so I don't know what kind of pictures we'll be able to get out of them.

Jim Lovell @JLCDRApollo13
Houston is asking us for battery readings every 15 minutes now. They need to understand that we have to maintain a work/rest cycle up here.

Jim Lovell @JLCDRApollo13
We can't just wait around here to take down detailed procedures all the time up to the burn.

Jack Swigert @JSCMPApollo13
I'm going to try and clean off the windows and do the best I can with the 250-millimeter lens on the Hasselblad camera.

Jim Lovell @JLCDRApollo13
We've got to get the procedures up here rapidly, look at them, figure out any problems and then get the people to sleep. The guys in Houston need to take that into consideration when they send up so many procedures.

Jack Swigert @JSCMPApollo13
Voltage is now 39.1, amps 1.75. We're having big problems hearing Houston right now. This is the last thing we need at this stage when we really need to be able to note down their detailed procedures.

Ken Mattingly @KMLMPilotApollo13
The mid-course burn should be at re-entry minus 5 hours.

Ken Mattingly @KMLMPilotApollo13
At re-entry minus 4 hours 30 minutes, we will need to verify that the lunar module is correctly configured for jettisoning from the command module.

5 days 7 hours mission time

Ken Mattingly @KMLMPilotApollo13
After the separation of the service module, there are several lunar module steps to be carried out before it separates from the command module.

Ken Mattingly @KMLMPilotApollo13
This was never envisaged for this stage in the mission, but we have practiced it a few times in the simulator now.

Ken Mattingly @KMLMPilotApollo13
When the service module has been jettisoned, the command module needs to pitch up and acquire the service module for photography of whatever damage there is on the vehicle.

Gene Kranz @GKFlgtDirApollo13
When they are down to reentry minus 3 hours, the next time event is when the lunar module should start a maneuver we are calling the Moon view attitude.

Gene Kranz @GKFlgtDirApollo13
This maneuver is designed to place the command module optics pointing directly at the Moon.

Ken Mattingly @KMLMPilotApollo13
The alignment for re-entry is likely to be most successful by aligning with the Moon. However, we have also sent up procedures for aligning with the Sun and any star systems they can recognize.

Gene Kranz @GKFlgtDirApollo13
If they are unable to use the sextant for the procedure, they can use the telescope, using the safety filters when taking readings from the Sun.

Ken Mattingly @KMLMPilotApollo13
We don't insist on them aligning with the Moon and maybe the Earth. If they can find good stars, they should use them.

Ken Mattingly @KMLMPilotApollo13
Close-out and hatch installation of the command module should be at re-entry minus 1 hour 30 minutes. Jettisoning of Aquarius, the lunar module, should be at re-entry minus 1 hour.

Gene Kranz @GKFlgtDirApollo13
At reentry minus 45 minus they will maneuver to the optimum angle for reentry using the Moon and the Earth as reference points through the sextant or telescope.

Jack Swigert @JSCMPApollo13
Ken says he thinks they have got all the little surprises ironed out for us. I sure hope so, because tomorrow is final examination time.

Vance Brand @VBrandCAPCOM
Much of the very detailed service module and lunar module separation and mid-course burn procedures has now been sent up despite the comms problems.

Vance Brand @VBrandCAPCOM
I just hope they got all the separation and burn procedures down correctly; there was an awful of it, to be carried out in a very short amount of time.

Vance Brand @VBrandCAPCOM
Amazingly, out of the masses of non-stop instructions and improvised procedures Ken Mattingly sent the astronauts, only one query was generated from all those gathered here in Mission Control.

Deke Slayton @DKDrctrFlghtCrwOps
After we send up the battery charging backout procedure, Jack needs to get some sleep. He's sure going to need it tomorrow.

Vance Brand @VBrandCAPCOM
Jim asked if we have any more updates. I told him that Freddo can handle anything else we have and that Jack and he ought to work as hard as he can at getting some sleep for the next 5 hours.

128 hours 26 minutes mission time
14 hours 12 minutes to re-entry

Walter Cronkite @WCronkiteCBSNews
The next critical moments come tomorrow morning. Just about 7 a.m. eastern time.

Walter Cronkite @WCronkiteCBSNews
The astronauts will climb back into their command ship and once again turn its power on—power that has been down, except for intermittent tests, since Monday night's explosion.

Walter Cronkite @WCronkiteCBSNews
That power has to work, and the astronauts and everyone at Mission Control will breathe a lot easier if it does.

Walter Cronkite @WCronkiteCBSNews
Just before 8.30 a.m., they'll jettison the long-dead service module and two and a half hours later jettison the lunar module which has been their lifeboat back from the Moon.

Leo Krupp @LKruppNARockwell
The critical pre-entry activity begins about 4 and a half hours before scheduled splashdown.

Leo Krupp @LKruppNARockwell
The command module must be separated from the service module in such a manner that there's no danger of further contact between the two.

Leo Krupp @LKruppNARockwell
The separation must be done delicately enough so that the homeward bound trajectory of the two remaining modules is not disturbed. It will take teamwork from both the command module and the lunar module.

Leo Krupp @LKruppNARockwell
After all three astronauts are in the command module, the separation from the lunar module will

occur about one hour before they enter the Earth's atmosphere.

Leo Krupp @LKruppNARockwell
At this time, hopefully the command module's systems will be all powered up. The tunnel hatch will be back in place and left pressurized.

Leo Krupp @LKruppNARockwell
When they are ready to separate, they will throw two switches and the pressure that's in the tunnel will force the two vehicles apart.

Walter Cronkite @WCronkiteCBSNews
A couple of hours after the lunar module drifts off from the command module, the command module will plunge through the Earth's atmosphere, hopefully to a splashdown in the Pacific.

Walter Cronkite @WCronkiteCBSNews
The weather in the splashdown area is said to be good tonight, and besides the recovery ship the USS Iwo Jima, four Russian ships are said to be nearby.

Walter Cronkite @WCronkiteCBSNews
If you are Mary Haise, expecting your fourth child this summer, you try to avoid the anxiety by going to the home of a friend.

Walter Cronkite @WCronkiteCBSNews
In this case today, along with Marilyn Lovell, the get-together was at chief astronaut Deke Slayton's house.

Walter Cronkite @WCronkiteCBSNews
Later, both wives posed for pictures but did not answer reporters' questions. If the flight had been

normal, they might have been talking about their husbands' walk on the Moon. But... it was not to be.

Walter Cronkite @WCronkiteCBSNews
In Denver, the parents of bachelor astronaut Jack Swigert said they were feeling encouraged following last night's successful mid-course correction burn.

Walter Cronkite @WCronkiteCBSNews
Russia's cosmonauts sent a message to the Apollo 13 astronauts today saying, "We are following your flight with great attention and anxiety. We wish you wholeheartedly a safe return to our mother Earth."

David Brinkley @DBNBCNews
Apollo 13 continues on its approach to Earth. The astronauts are cold but still safe, speeding towards the Earth at more than 4,000 mph.

David Brinkley @DBNBCNews
The low temperature in the spacecraft is caused by a reluctance to use electricity for heat.

David Brinkley @DBNBCNews
One of the astronauts told Mission Control here in Houston this afternoon, "It is like living in a refrigerator."

David Brinkley @DBNBCNews
Much of the astronauts' day was spent today getting detailed instructions from Mission Control on tomorrow's maneuvers.

David Brinkley @DBNBCNews
The instructions the astronauts have been carefully noting down are detailed and complicated because

the sequence of events to be carried out in space tomorrow has never been carried out before.

David Brinkley @DBNBCNews
The troubles of Apollo 13 have not shaken the confidence of other astronauts, at least not in public. Many of them have publicly stated their confidence in the space program.

Neil Armstrong @NArmstrongNASA
We expect a certain amount of these things to occur and it's no big surprise. In fact, it's more of a surprise when things run perfectly well as they did on Apollo 11.

Neil Armstrong @NArmstrongNASA
I'm still somewhat amazed that things worked so well during our Moon mission.

Neil Armstrong @NArmstrongNASA
When these things do happen, they're usually a bit different than anything we ever prepared for.

Neil Armstrong @NArmstrongNASA
I don't fault the design engineers or the test teams in this case. I'm sure it was just one of those million-to-one shots that you can't prepare for.

Fred Haise @FHLMPilotApollo13
Jim and Jack are trying to sleep now. Meanwhile, Houston have some more lunar module procedures to read to me. They say I'll need several pages to note it all down and should be prepared to get writer's cramp.

Fred Haise @FHLMPilotApollo13
If I don't seem too clear talking to Houston right now, that's because I'm talking while holding a flashlight between my teeth while I write down all these procedures.

Fred Haise @FHLMPilotApollo13
More procedures are coming up now.

Jim Lovell @JLCDRApollo13
Can't sleep. So many steps and procedures just to get rid of a lunar module that's going to burn up in the atmosphere a half hour after it is jettisoned. Much of it seems superfluous.

Jim Lovell @JLCDRApollo13
We need to be looking at only the essential things to do to ensure a safe lunar module jettison.

Jim Lovell @JLCDRApollo13
Doing that alignment on the Earth at the planned time in these conditions is going to be really tricky, like landing an aircraft with a fogged-up windshield.

Jim Lovell @JLCDRApollo13
I don't think we have the time to get all the engineering data people in Mission Control might want to look at as Aquarius goes into the atmosphere.

Jim Lovell @JLCDRApollo13
We'll do everything they think is essential, but I don't want to be throwing switches at the last minute. What we're really thinking about is just getting Odyssey into good shape as a re-entry vehicle.

Vance Brand @VBrandCAPCOM
Jimbo needs to go back to sleep and stop worrying. To help him do that, we're sending up some of his favorite guitar music—12 string guitar of course.

Alan Bean @ABeanApollo12
We are extremely hopeful, and pretty confident, that the presently powerless and cold command module can be powered up sufficient to perform the tasks it has to do.

Alan Bean @ABeanApollo12
North American has been running a number of tests, as we have here, and we have determined that the craft, its electrical systems and many of the components can be powered up to an acceptable level for re-entry.

Jules Bergman @JBABCNews
Intensive simulations carried out by other astronauts on the ground these last few days say it should work. And it has to. Re-entry can't be delayed and there can be no second attempts.

Jules Bergman @JBABCNews
Once they have separated from the lunar module, the astronauts have only a few hours of oxygen and electrical power left.

Jules Bergman @JBABCNews
Those brave men up in space will have only one shot at attempting a successful re-entry.

Jules Bergman @JBABCNews
During re-entry, the spacecraft must survive the intense heat generated as the capsule plunges through the Earth's atmosphere and hope that their

heat shield was not damaged in the explosion and can protect them.

David Brinkley @DBNBCNews
The re-entry and recovery schedule for tomorrow is: the small mid-course correction comes at 7.53 a.m. At 8.23, they'll jettison the service module. At 10.23, they'll transfer all power over to the command module.

David Brinkley @DBNBCNews
At 11.53, they'll jettison the lunar module. At 12.53, they'll enter the Earth's interface. At 1.01 p.m., the drogue chutes should deploy, and at 1.07 p.m. eastern standard time, they should splashdown into the Pacific.

129 hours 32 minutes mission time
13 hours 6 minutes to re-entry

Vance Brand @VBrandCAPCOM
We're going to try to refrain from calling Freddo from now on so that he can maybe get a couple of winks.

Gene Kranz @GKFlgtDirApollo13
The time between 2 hours 30 minutes and 1 hour before reentry is going to be real busy for the crew and they're really going to have to hustle to get everything done.

Jack Swigert @JSCMPApollo13
Just woke up. I got between 2 and 3 hours sleep. It was awful cold and it wasn't very good sleep. Too much to think about.

Gene Kranz @GKFlgtDirApollo13
All three crew really should try to get whatever sleep they can. They have just 2 to 3 hours before they really have to get at it.

Deke Slayton @DKDrctrFlghtCrwOps
I wish we could figure out a way to get a cup of hot coffee up to the crew. It would probably taste pretty good right now.

David Brinkley @DBNBCNews
Here in Houston, there's a suburb called Clear Lake. It is home to astronauts Jim Lovell, Fred Haise and many other astronauts and their families.

David Brinkley @DBNBCNews
If there is any tension about Apollo 13, it is not readily seen here. But as in all of Houston, there is deep concern.

David Brinkley @DBNBCNews
NASA says Marilyn Lovell has asked few questions. She doesn't need to. They say she is knowledgable.

David Brinkley @DBNBCNews
Mrs Mary Haise, who is expecting their fourth child in two months, went to have lunch with the wife of astronaut Alan Beam today.

David Brinkley @DBNBCNews
Both wives have been visiting, and been visited by, the wives of other astronauts because that's the way it works here in Houston.

David Brinkley @DBNBCNews
Last night in the Astrodome, Houston played Los Angeles and the thousands of fans took note of the

President's request for silent prayer for the Apollo 13 astronauts. This in a stadium not known for silence.

Jules Bergman @JBABCNews
The mid-course correction burn tonight is critical. Apollo 13 on the course it's currently flying will miss the Earth by 94 miles.

Jules Bergman @JBABCNews
Ironically, if all had gone well, the lunar module would have landed on the Moon tonight and Jim Lovell and Fred Haise would be performing their first moonwalk right now.

Jules Bergman @JBABCNews
Instead, the astronauts are limping across space in their lunar module with a crippled command/service module in tow.

Jules Bergman @JBABCNews
The astronauts are alive only because they have been able to improvise systems to save their lives with brilliant on the spot help from the ground in Houston.

Gene Kranz @GKFlgtDirApollo13
We know the crew are having great difficulty sleeping due to the cold and anxiety, so we've advised that they pull out the medical kit and pop a couple of Dexedrines just prior to when things really start to get busy.

133 hours 22 minutes mission time
9 hours 6 minutes to re-entry

Jim Lovell @JLCDRApollo13
The next few hours sure are going to be interesting to say the least. The Earth is a lot bigger now and the crescent is a lot more pronounced than it was just a few hours ago.

Gene Kranz @GKFlgtDirApollo13
One way for the crew to warm things up in a hurry is when they turn on their AC, to also turn on the window heaters.

Jim Lovell @JLCDRApollo13
It's getting a little warmer in here now. That is much appreciated. The Sun feels wonderful. It's shining in the rendezvous window.

Jim Lovell @JLCDRApollo13
I'm trying to get a check on the Moon to see if our angles are indeed true. We got the Moon back again and centered.

Jim Lovell @JLCDRApollo13
The stars Denebola and Regulus are nearby so we're taking a check off them. I've got Sirius too. That's a nice one. How about that?

Jim Lovell @JLCDRApollo13
I'm pitching over now, trying to pick up another star. Sirius was just too far off. I thought I was going to use too much gas getting there.

Gene Kranz @GKFlgtDirApollo13
We think we've figured out a way to save the crew some time during a very critical period. That's by

doing an alignment while they are still docked. That will save them a maneuver or two.

Gene Kranz @GKFlgtDirApollo13
It'll save them a bit of time during a period when they're going to be very, very busy. It'll also save them some petrol.

Jack Swigert @JSCMPApollo13
Hey, it's really warmed up here now. It's almost comfortable.

Jim Lovell @JLCDRApollo13
I'm looking out the window now and the Earth is whistling in like a high-speed freight train. Houston say we are now just 48,000 miles out.

136 hours 5 minutes mission time
6 hours 33 minutes to re-entry

Gene Kranz @GKFlgtDirApollo13
We have sent up the lunar module roll, pitch and yaw coordinates. Also the command module's coordinates which they will have to maneuver into at one hour before re-entry.

Joe Kerwin @JKerwinCAPCOM
We have handed the computer back to the astronauts. Jack is doing the lunar module pre-heat and reports a voltage drop of 2 volts on the meter.

Deke Slayton @DKDrctrFlghtCrwOps
I'm told the crew have broken out the medical kit and taken the Dexedrine tablets as we suggested. I'm now recommending that they hit the medical kit and Dexedrine again in about 2 hours.

Joe Kerwin @JKerwinCAPCOM
We are now registering that Apollo 13 is nearly, but not quite, in the right attitude for the burn. Jim is still maneuvering the spacecraft. Oh, wait...

Jim Lovell @JLCDRApollo13
Houston is telling me that we're rolled the wrong way. How did that happen?

Joe Kerwin @JKerwinCAPCOM
Okay, Jim got a handle on it. Attitude is looking much better now. We'll give them a mark at 10 minutes to the burn.

Jim Lovell @JLCDRApollo13
About 3 minutes to go to the burn and we're all squared away.

Joe Kerwin @JKerwinCAPCOM
Apollo 13 is GO for burn.

Fred Haise @FHLMPilotApollo13
We're burning.

Jim Lovell @JLCDRApollo13
20%... 40%..

Jim Lovell @JLCDRApollo13
60%... 80%...

Jim Lovell @JLCDRApollo13
Shut down. Burn completed.

Jim Lovell @JLCDRApollo13
Jack just reported that the thrusters fired on both rings. Looks like it was a fine burn.

Charlie Duke @CDukeNASA
Lots of applause down here for what looks to have been an excellent final burn and course correction to put them into the correct attitude for re-entry.

Jim Lovell @JLCDRApollo13
That's a great relief. It was pretty much a 'white-knuckle' job holding things steady during that final burn.

Jim Lovell @JLCDRApollo13
We will now maneuver into position to jettison the service module and try to photograph the damage on the craft caused by the explosion or whatever it was.

137 hours 47 minutes mission time
5 hours 51 minutes to re-entry

Gene Kranz @GKFlgtDirApollo13
Service module jettison is now set for 138 hours 12 minutes flight time. But actually it's not that time-critical. They could jettison the service module at any time before then.

Jim Lovell @JLCDRApollo13
I'm now pitching up to the proper attitude. It's not easy, not easy at all but as soon as we get rid of the service module, I think I'll be able to maneuver a lot better.

Jim Lovell @JLCDRApollo13
Separating from the service module now.

Fred Haise @FHLMPilotApollo13
We can see the service module drifting away.

Jim Lovell @JLCDRApollo13
Wow! There's one whole side of that spacecraft missing.

Jim Lovell @JLCDRApollo13
Right by the high-gain antenna, the whole panel is blown out, almost from the base to the engine.

Joe Kerwin @JKerwinCAPCOM
We've asked the crew to get whatever pictures of the damaged service module they can, but not to make any unnecessary maneuvers.

Actual Apollo 13 photo of the damaged service module

Fred Haise @FHLMPilotApollo13
Looks like the explosion zinged the engine bell, too. Man, that's unbelievable. It really is a mess!

Jim Lovell @JLCDRApollo13
I can see a lot of debris just hanging out the side, near the S-band antenna.

Joe Kerwin @JKerwinCAPCOM
I just told Jim that if he can't take better care of a spacecraft than that, we might not give him another one.

Jack Swigert @JSCMPApollo13
I have a problem here. I can't get the computer to go into standby mode. I just get a flashing light somewhere else, but no standby light.

Ken Mattingly @KMLMPilotApollo13
Jack says he held down the computer standby button for 2 or 3 seconds. We think it may need to be held down to up to half a minute or more now due to the reduced power.

Wally Schirra @WSchirraNASA
Now that the re-entry vehicle is detached from the service module, it becomes exposed to the extreme cold of space. One of the reasons NASA insisted on remaining attached for so long was to protect that shield.

Wally Schirra @WSchirraNASA
The hope now is that the heat shield was not damaged in the explosion and that the remaining hours in the extreme cold will not result in any cracking of the shield.

138 hours 20 minutes mission time
4 hours 18 minutes to re-entry

Jim Lovell @JLCDRApollo13
Battery C current is now 2 amps. Battery A voltage is 30.2, so we're OK there.

Gene Kranz @GKFlgtDirApollo13
We need half up to an amp less current than the crew are reporting. Jack needs to check the circuit breakers and switches he's pulled so far to make sure that he doesn't have any extra loads on the batteries.

Jack Swigert @JSCMPApollo13
Computer is working fine now, just needed to hold down the button until it came on. I've turned off the floodlights but I'm not reading any voltage at all on battery C.

Ken Mattingly @KMLMPilotApollo13
Jack should be able to use the floodlight levels we gave him. There's no reason to sit in the dark. The floodlight power should be coming off battery B.

Ken Mattingly @KMLMPilotApollo13
Joe is reading more reentry procedures up to Jim in the command module. A mass of data about Moon, Earth and stars alignments; roll pitch and yaw positioning, etc. Also, landing area details.

Gene Kranz @GKFlgtDirApollo13
In the mid-Pacific landing area, the weather is good. Visibility is 10 miles, waves are 4 feet. Scattered showers in 10% of the area.

Gene Kranz @GKFlgtDirApollo13
The USS Iwo Jima will be at the touchdown point. The aircraft call sign will be Recovery-1 with swimmers on board. We have the backup landing area covered with the USS Hall.

Jim Lovell @JLCDRApollo13
The carrier Iwo Jima is to be our prime recovery ship—great!

Jim Lovell @JLCDRApollo13
The voltage on battery A is now up to 31.0—also great.

Jim Lovell @JLCDRApollo13
Jack tells me he's having difficulty getting a fix on the stars with the sextant. I'm going to pitch up a little to see if I can get him into a better viewing spot.

Jim Lovell @JLCDRApollo13
It feels real nice to be able to use the hand controller again without having the service module pulling us off balance all the time.

Joe Kerwin @JKerwinCAPCOM
To get a better fix on the stars, we're recommending Jim navigate to a different attitude than the one we sent in the last update. We're sending up the new coordinates now.

Ken Mattingly @KMLMPilotApollo13
We had computed that the stars Vega, Altair, Rasalhague and Daneb would all be in the sextant/telescope field of view. Jack should be able to see at least one of those four stars now.

139 hours 15 minutes mission time
3 hours 23 minutes to re-entry

Ken Mattingly @KMLMPilotApollo13
With the amount of power they have in the lunar module now, at the rate they are using power, they have about 12 hours of power left. Looks like they will make it through on the power front.

Jim Lovell @JLCDRApollo13
Twelve hours of power left is enough for two re-entry attempts. Pity we only get to have one go at it.

Jim Lovell @JLCDRApollo13
Jack reported that he thinks he can see Altair. I went back there to take a look and it looks pretty grim. We may have to do some fine align docking angles if we have time.

Jim Lovell @JLCDRApollo13
One problem here is that there are all kinds of bright objects floating around us. It's just reflecting like mad. We can give it a try though—if we see Altair, we'll get it.

Ken Mattingly @KMLMPilotApollo13
In the event the crew are unable to get a fix on the stars, we're standing by with the original scheme, a set of angles to fly to that'll point the command module optics at the Moon and the Sun.

Ken Mattingly @KMLMPilotApollo13
If Jack is unable to see the stars, Jim will have to maneuver the craft to the Moon-viewing attitude and then the Sun-viewing attitude.

Ken Mattingly @KMLMPilotApollo13
If we run out of time for using the stars, Sun or Moon, the course align angles they will need to implement are: ROLL plus 298.95, PITCH 271.38, YAW plus 000.28.

139 hours 51 minutes flight time
2 hours 38 minutes to re-entry

Gene Kranz @GKFlgtDirApollo13
Apollo 13 is now GO for powering up the command module. Doing it with procedures that normally take 3 months to figure out, but were completed by the teams down here in under 3 days!

Jim Lovell @JLCDRApollo13
Fred is with Jack powering up the command module. I'm staying down here in good old Aquarius—our lifeboat throughout most of this hair-raising journey.

Jack Swigert @JSCMPApollo13
The command module is in pretty bad shape... cold and clammy. The walls, ceiling and floor are covered in tiny droplets of water.

Jack Swigert @JSCMPApollo13
I'm worried that conditions might be the same behind all the panels. There must be a good chance all this water is going to cause arcing and short circuits. Nothing we can do about it now though.

Joe Kerwin @JKerwinCAPCOM
We're not yet able to establish communications between the command module and Mission Control down here. We're not reading Odyssey at all.

Jim Lovell @JLCDRApollo13
In order to rely instructions from Houston between Aquarius and the command module, I have instituted a new onboard communication system.

Jim Lovell @JLCDRApollo13
The technical term for this system is to be known as 'Yelling through the tunnel'.

140 hours 23 minutes flight time
2 hours 15 minutes to re-entry

Fred Haise @FHLMPilotApollo13
We have current on battery B, but I'm unable to read any voltage.

Joe Kerwin @JKerwinCAPCOM
The reason Fred is unable to read any voltage is we have a circuit breaker there that we have called as being out. The computer is now with Jack.

Joe Kerwin @JKerwinCAPCOM
We're coming up on time for the course align, so Jim needs to hold his attitude real good.

Jack Swigert @JSCMPApollo13
I have another alarm going off—last thing we need at this point with so little time left.

Jim Lovell @JLCDRApollo13
Working on the fine course align now. I think I've just about got it... Yes!

Jim Lovell @JLCDRApollo13
We have completed the course align. We're now maneuvering to the attitude to jettison the Aquarius lunar module into the Earth's atmosphere.

Jack Swigert @JSCMPApollo13
I'm trying to get a fix on Vega and Altair through the telescope, but my view is obscured by all that stuff that vented from the service module and is still surrounding us.

Jim Lovell @JLCDRApollo13
I have a warning light, too. But Houston tell me it's just low helium; so no sweat I guess.

Jack Swigert @JSCMPApollo13
Finally, I've captured usable some star angles through the sextant. We're now maneuvering to the Aquarius-jettisoning attitude.

140 hours 55 minutes flight time
1 hour 43 minutes to re-entry

Jim Lovell @JLCDRApollo13
We're having trouble maneuvering without getting the craft in gimbal lock. Houston sure picked a lousy attitude for this separation.

Jim Lovell @JLCDRApollo13
I'm now finally at the lunar module separation attitude and am thinking of bailing out.

Joe Kerwin @JKerwinCAPCOM
We need Jim to verify that the hatch between Aquarius and the command module is now secured, and that they are venting the tunnel.

Gene Kranz @GKFlgtDirApollo13
We have had verification that the hatch between the two crafts is now secured and Apollo 13 is now GO

for separation from lunar module Aquarius at their convenience.

141 hours 22 minutes flight time
1 hour 16 minutes to re-entry

Jack Swigert @JSCMPApollo13
About to let go of Aquarius. We'll punch off at 141 hours 30 minutes.

Jack Swigert @JSCMPApollo13
Ten seconds... ...five...

Jack Swigert @JSCMPApollo13
three...two...

Jack Swigert @JSCMPApollo13
I have confirmed lunar module separation and jettison.

Joe Kerwin @JKerwinCAPCOM
Farewell, Aquarius, and we thank you.

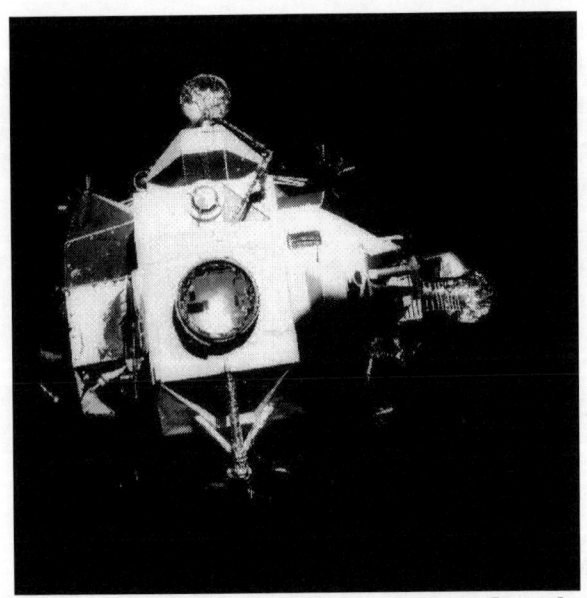

The lunar module Aquarius just after being jettisoned from the command module

Joe Kerwin @JKerwinCAPCOM
Jack did a good job on the sextant star reading. It checks out down here, so we're giving him a gold star on that one.

Jack Swigert @JSCMPApollo13
All three of us just sent down a big thank you to all the guys down there in Mission Control for the very fine job they did. It really was quite an heroic effort on their part.

Wally Schirra @WSchirraNASA
The lunar module Aquarius was built by the guys at Grumman Aerospace. I'm hearing they are drafting an invoice for $400,540 and 5 cents for 'towing fees' for dragging our crippled ship most of the way to the Moon and back.

Wally Schirra @WSchirraNASA
That figure is based on an estimated 400,001 miles at $1 per mile. An extra $536.05 has been included for battery-charging, oxygen and the accommodation of an additional guest in the room.

Wally Schirra @WSchirraNASA
They're just joking there…. At least I think they are.

142 hours 6 minutes flight time
32 minutes to re-entry

Gene Kranz @GKFlgtDirApollo13
It looks as though battery C will deplete around main chute time. However, Apollo 13 is still looking fat on power. We have them at 30 amp hours remaining when they hit water.

Gene Kranz @GKFlgtDirApollo13
If they're not picked up by the recovery helicopters immediately, they can put the pyro batteries online if they need them after they're down.

Jack Swigert @JSCMPApollo13
Sure wish I could go to the Mission Control party tonight. It's likely to be a wild one. If those guys need any phone numbers from the NASA bachelor, I'll be more than happy to pass them over from the recovery vessel.

Joe Kerwin @JKerwinCAPCOM
Lost contact with Apollo 13 for a few minutes there. Fortunately, we're back in touch with the astronauts now.

Gene Kranz @GKFlgtDirApollo13
Apollo 13 is still looking good. Trajectory is fine. The crew want to know if we're still tracking Aquarius.

Gene Kranz @GKFlgtDirApollo13
The crew seem to have formed an emotional bond to lunar module Aquarius. Who can blame them? She sure was a fine ship... did a fantastic job for those guys.

Gene Kranz @GKFlgtDirApollo13
We just picked up a signal from Aquarius, so it seems she's still ticking out there somewhere. Such a shame she'll be burning up in the Earth's atmosphere shortly.

142 hours 31 minutes flight time
7 minutes to re-entry

Joe Kerwin @JKerwinCAPCOM
We just had one final time around the room and everybody says Apollo 13 is looking great. Still crossing our fingers though and sweating not a little.

Joe Kerwin @JKerwinCAPCOM
Nobody wants to speak about the heat shield. No point – we can't do anything about it.

Gene Kranz @GKFlgtDirApollo13
Ten minutes to re-entry interface.

Gene Kranz @GKFlgtDirApollo13
Five minutes.

142 hours 37 minutes flight time
1 minute to re-entry

Joe Kerwin @JKerwinCAPCOM
We're looking at the weather on TV and it looks just as advertised, real good. Apollo 13 will be hitting the atmosphere right around now.

Jules Bergman @JBABCNews
As the spacecraft plummets through the atmosphere, the heat shield will have to survive over 4,000 degrees of heat.

Jules Bergman @JBABCNews
If the heat shield was even slightly cracked in the explosion, the intense cold of the voyage could have split it wide open. Nobody knows at this point.

Gene Kranz @GKFlgtDirApollo13
The re-entry vehicle is now punching its way through the Earth's atmosphere. This is the most tense time.

Gene Kranz @GKFlgtDirApollo13
I believe even the atheists among us are issuing silent prayers right now.

Jules Bergman @JBABCNews
If the pyrotechnics that control the parachutes were damaged in the explosion, the chutes may not open at all causing the spacecraft to hit the water at a suicidal 300 m.p.h.

Joe Kerwin @JKerwinCAPCOM
Now for two or three minutes of absolute torture while we wait for the usual radio blackout period to end while the capsule hurtles through the atmosphere.

Jim Lovell @JLCDRApollo13
Unbelievable! While we are entering the Earth's atmosphere, it is actually raining here inside the command module.

Jack Swigert @JSCMPApollo13
As we are going through the intense heat of re-entry, all the frozen water droplets on the command module's walls and ceiling are rapidly melting and raining down on us. Incredible!

Walter Cronkite @WCronkiteCBSNews
The heat shield right now will be burning at nearly 5,000 degrees and much of it will actually melt away due to the intense heat and end up as a charred mess.

Walter Cronkite @WCronkiteCBSNews
Everyone is praying that the heat shield will hold and protect the astronauts from the searing heat of re-entry through the atmosphere.

Walter Cronkite @WCronkiteCBSNews
In a short while, the drogue chute should deploy first and pull out the three main chutes.

Wally Schirra @WSchirraNASA
The drogue chute deployment will provide breaking and stabilization prior to main chutes deployment.

Joe Kerwin @JKerwinCAPCOM
We are continuing to monitor. Nine minutes to scheduled splashdown.

Walter Cronkite @WCronkiteCBSNews
The period of blackout for the spacecraft should have begun some 20 or so odd seconds ago.

Walter Cronkite @WCronkiteCBSNews
No re-entry vehicle has ever taken longer than 3 minutes to emerge from radio blackout. This is the critical moment. Will the heat shield hold? If it doesn't... there will only be silence.

Gene Kranz @GKFlgtDirApollo13
Apollo 13 should be coming up on maximum G-force right now. We have about a minute and a half to go during blackout.

Joe Kerwin @JKerwinCAPCOM
Waiting to regain contact with Apollo 13.

Walter Cronkite @WCronkiteCBSNews
There are now wall-to-wall people crammed into Grand Central Station in New York watching the landing on a giant TV screen there.

Walter Cronkite @WCronkiteCBSNews
The silence there is palpable at this time as it is in Mission Control, Houston and indeed in our TV studio here.

Wally Schirra @WSchirraNASA
The scenes from the recovery ship Iwo Jima are now being flashed up on one of the large screens in Mission Control for the flight controllers to watch.

Wally Schirra @WSchirraNASA
About 30 seconds to go to the end of radio blackout.

Joe Kerwin @JKerwinCAPCOM
Two minutes since last contact. Still no signal.

Joe Kerwin @JKerwinCAPCOM
Two minutes 30 seconds. Waiting for signal from Apollo 13.

Joe Kerwin @JKerwinCAPCOM
Three minutes...

Walter Cronkite @WCronkiteCBSNews
We're looking at the weather on TV and it looks just as good as advertised... real good.

Walter Cronkite @WCronkiteCBSNews
Apollo 13 should be coming out of blackout at this time with 7 minutes to splashdown if the heat shield has held and the parachutes have deployed.

Joe Kerwin @JKerwinCAPCOM
Apollo 13 should be out of blackout at this time. We are standing by for any reports of Orion aircraft acquisition.

Joe Kerwin @JKerwinCAPCOM
Four minutes since loss of signal.

Walter Cronkite @WCronkiteCBSNews
We ought to be hearing something around now. They should have been out of that blackout a minute and 15 seconds ago.

Joe Kerwin @JKerwinCAPCOM
Coming up now on 5 minutes since end of blackout. Standing by for any reports of acquisition. We will attempt to contact through one of the Orion aircraft.

Walter Cronkite @WCronkiteCBSNews
Those controllers have done their work to the best of their ability and now all they can do is sit and watch and wait, along with a great deal of the rest of humanity.

Walter Cronkite @WCronkiteCBSNews
Looking at the screen, scanning for any sign of parachutes now.

Gene Kranz @GKFlgtDirApollo13
Five minutes plus. You could hear a pin drop here at Mission Control.

Mission controllers watching the large screen in Mission Control and waiting to hear a signal from Apollo 13

Joe Kerwin @JKerwinCAPCOM
Six minutes since loss of contact...

Joe Kerwin @JKerwinCAPCOM
Coming up on seven minutes... This is hard to bear!

Joe Kerwin @JKerwinCAPCOM
Ok, we have them!!!

Joe Kerwin @JKerwinCAPCOM
We have them on the big screen! Reading Jack now!

Wally Schirra @WSchirraNASA
I just heard Jack Swigert come through with, "OK Joe!".

Jack Swigert @JSCMPApollo13
We have good drogue parachutes bringing us down smoothly.

Swim Team 2 @ST2IwoJima
We're in the recovery helicopter and I have a visual bearing on the capsule and parachutes. Seeing them going through 5,000 feet. Chutes look good.

Walter Cronkite @WCronkiteCBSNews
There is huge commotion on the deck of the USS Iwo Jima now as some the ship's crew say they have caught a glimpse of Apollo 13 descending through the high clouds.

Swim Team 2 @ST2IwoJima
Apollo 13 is now descending through 2,000 feet.

Walter Cronkite @WCronkiteCBSNews
The floor of the Mission Control operations room is now crowded with cheering NASA technicians and controllers as Apollo 13 continues to descend through several banks of light cloud.

Swim Team 2 @ST2IwoJima
1,000 feet.

Wally Schirra @WSchirraNASA
Look at that! That's the best sight... the three main chutes open and successfully bringing down Apollo 13.

Walter Cronkite @WCronkiteCBSNews
Just one more minute to splashdown according to Mission Control, Houston. What amazing pictures! Look at that! We are also listening to the conversation between the recovery helicopter and the crew of Apollo 13.

Richard O'Brian @RBCBSNews
I'm on the carrier Iwo Jima and can clearly see Apollo 13 coming down just exactly where they said it would. The calculation is the capsule is 4 miles dead ahead, so it should be just a perfect pickup here.

Walter Cronkite @WCronkiteCBSNews
The pictures we are seeing now are being broadcast live from the recovery helicopter.

Walter Cronkite @WCronkiteCBSNews
Broad smiles on the face of everyone at Mission Control. There will be a lot of big fat cigars lit there shortly in Mission Control I can tell you that.

Richard O'Brian @RBCBSNews
We can see the helicopter teams moving in now as Apollo 13 glides smoothly down into the Pacific Ocean.

Richard O'Brian @RBCBSNews
Just now, I can see smoke coming from the capsule and drifting upwards. I have no idea what that is.

Wally Schirra @WSchirraNASA
The venting we can see on the screen right now is a little venting of fuel as the capsule descends. The crew are expelling RCS propellant—reaction control system propellant, as an added safety precaution at this time.

Walter Cronkite @WCronkiteCBSNews
The massed crowds in New York and all the mission controllers in Houston are erupting now in spontaneous applause and loud cheering. What a sight on that large TV screen! What a moment!

Swim Team 2 @ST2IwoJima
Through 500 feet. Swim teams 1 and 2 are on station.

The descent as seen by the controllers in Mission Control

Gene Kranz @GKFlgtDirApollo13
What a wonderful sight! Words cannot express how I feel right now, but I believe bringing home these men home will come to be seen as NASA's 'finest hour'.

Ken Mattingly @KMLMPilotApollo13
While Gene Kranz and his team are going to get much of the deserved credit, we must never forget the role played by Glynne Lunney and his team.

Ken Mattingly @KMLMPilotApollo13
In my opinion, as flight controller of 'Black Team', Glynne Lunney's performance during the worst moments of the crisis was the most magnificent display of personal leadership that I have ever seen.

Photo Chopper 1 @PHIwoJima
Photo 1 observes splashdown at this time.

Jim Lovell @JLCDRApollo13
Oh, man! We made it! We made it and we are 'Stable 1'.

Swim Team 2 @ST2IwoJima
The three chutes are now displaced. They're in the water. Swim team 2 is about to enter the water and pick up our guys.

Richard O'Brian @RBCBSNews
The recovery helicopter is reporting that Apollo 13 is 'Stable One' and riding comfortably. 'Stable One' means the capsule is right side up.

David Brinkley @DBNBCNews
What great pictures! I've never seen anything like this before as the capsule bobs up and down and the three recovery helicopters approach. Looks more like a training exercise.

Walter Cronkite @WCronkiteCBSNews
Swells are reported to be 3 to 5 feet. You can see how the Apollo 13 command module is not a very good boat—a lot of bobbing and rocking action down there on the swells.

Richard O'Brian @RBCBSNews
The crew of Apollo13 have just reported to the carrier USS Iwo Jima that they are in very good shape inside the capsule. We must now wait a few moments before the divers begin their work of recovering the crew.

Walter Cronkite @WCronkiteCBSNews
Part of the delay as the recovery helicopters circle over the Apollo 13 capsule is to let the vehicle cool off. It has been heated up to 5,000 degrees so a little cooling off period is required.

Wally Schirra @WSchirraNASA
The divers will be in the water shortly, but one of the other things they are waiting for is for the three uprighting and stabilizing bags on top of the capsule to be fully inflated. They are currently one-third inflated.

Wally Schirra @WSchirraNASA
If the capsule had entered the water nose first, as has happened before, inflating those bags would have the effect of bringing the capsule into an upright position on the water.

Wally Schirra @WSchirraNASA
Right now, those inflating air bags are just giving the capsule additional stability.

Walter Cronkite @WCronkiteCBSNews
Okay. There they go. There go the divers leaping off the main recovery helicopter into the water right next to the Odyssey command module which continues to bob up and down and side to side quite a great deal.

Richard O'Brian @RBCBSNews
Uprighting bags are now 60% inflated. The first swimmer has now reached the command module.

Walter Cronkite @WCronkiteCBSNews
The huge crowds in Grand Central Terminal are still watching intently on the big screen... waiting for the first glimpse of these three heroic returning astronauts.

Wally Schirra @WSchirraNASA
We can see that the three uprighting/floatation bags on the top of the capsule are now fully inflated and the swimmers are working the floatation collar around the command module.

Wally Schirra @WSchirraNASA
The floatation collar will be pulled right around the command module before it is inflated.

Wally Schirra @WSchirraNASA
Shortly, two seven-man life rafts will be dropped from the helicopters with sea anchors attached to the bottom. This is done to keep the rafts from turning over from helicopter backwash.

Wally Schirra @WSchirraNASA
Jim Lovell has been requested to turn off the flashing beacon atop the capsule.

Wally Schirra @WSchirraNASA
We joke that the last thing the command module commander has to do before leaving the capsule is to turn off all the lights, but it's actually quite important.

Wally Schirra @WSchirraNASA
The commander turns off all the electrically-powered systems inside the command module so that what little electrical power that remains in the capsule can be calculated and the information used for future missions.

Walter Cronkite @WCronkiteCBSNews
We can see that the inflation collar is now fully inflated, so now there's no chance of this thing sinking or turning over.

Walter Cronkite @WCronkiteCBSNews
One of the divers is now standing on the floatation collar and has signaled to one of the helicopters to deploy the life rafts.

Walter Cronkite @WCronkiteCBSNews
Unlike on previous Apollo missions, this time there will be no delay in getting the men into the raft and then into the helicopter.

Walter Cronkite @WCronkiteCBSNews
There will be none of the scrubbing down, the decontamination procedures which were considered necessary for missions which successfully landed on the Moon.

Walter Cronkite @WCronkiteCBSNews
The astronauts will not be going into isolation for 3 weeks. Although I'm sure these three men would

have preferred to suffer the 3 weeks isolation having successfully completed their Moon landing.

Walter Cronkite @WCronkiteCBSNews
But... it was not to be. Not this time.

David Brinkley @DBNBCNews
The raft has now been dropped into the water—approximately 10 feet from the command module. The two swimmers have the raft in hand and are pulling it to the command module.

Walter Cronkite @WCronkiteCBSNews
The egress raft has now been inflated and we expect the next operation to be the opening of the hatch of the command module when we may get our first glimpse of three very relieved and tired astronauts.

Wally Schirra @WSchirraNASA
There are now 3 swimmers in the water. This recovery is going like clockwork. I'm very impressed with how this crew is working. It's a beautiful thing to watch.

Walter Cronkite @WCronkiteCBSNews
The rescue net is now being lowered from the helicopter. They're lowering that even before they open the hatch. Really picking up the tempo here. The helicopter is now maneuvering to place the rescue net in the egress raft.

Walter Cronkite @WCronkiteCBSNews
Something seems to be up as the helicopter has now pulled the rescue net back up and is rapidly backing away from the command module. Looks like there is some kind of problem.

Wally Schirra @WSchirraNASA
That's a new one on me and we're not hearing any word right now indicating what the problem might be.

Walter Cronkite @WCronkiteCBSNews
One of the swimmers is peaking in Odyssey's forward viewing window. He's now working the hatch.

Wally Schirra @WSchirraNASA
I can recall we designed this hatch after the Apollo 1 disaster. We were afraid the hatch would come roaring open and sweep the scuba divers right off the side.

David Brinkley @DBNBCNews
The hatch is now open. The swimmer has tossed something inside and closed the hatch again.

David Brinkley @DBNBCNews
I don't know what that is about, unless the astronauts want some clean clothes to wear and some privacy while they change into them.

Walter Cronkite @WCronkiteCBSNews
The hatch is open again and the first astronaut is climbing out of the command module, over the floatation collar and safely into the egress raft.

Walter Cronkite @WCronkiteCBSNews
Now the second astronaut... and here comes number three. All three astronauts are now safely in the egress raft waiting to be hoisted into the Recovery 1 helicopter.

Jim Lovell @JLCDRApollo13
Outside the Odyssey now. This ocean air sure smells good. Real good!... What a journey!

David Brinkley @DBNBCNews
The helicopter has now returned with the rescue net and the net has been placed firmly on the life raft. The first astronaut is climbing aboard and is now being winched into the helicopter.

David Brinkley @DBNBCNews
The first astronaut is now at the cargo hatch and is safely aboard the helicopter. Recovery 1 is reporting that the first astronaut is Fred Haise and that his condition is excellent.

Wally Schirra @WSchirraNASA
Both Fred Haise and Jack Swigert were space rookies on this flight. I'd say that after this mission they are well and truly veterans. This was quite a mission!

Wally Schirra @WSchirraNASA
Recovery 1 is now in position for the second retrieval. There goes the second astronaut up into the helicopter. Nice pickup... no oscillation.

Swim Team 2 @ST2IwoJima
We have astronaut Jack Swigert on board and he reports he feels fine.

David Brinkley @DBNBCNews
So Jim Lovell will be the final astronaut to be recovered. I suppose as commander that is appropriate. It may even be official stated NASA procedure.

Swim Team 2 @ST2IwoJima
Commander Jim Lovell is now aboard Recovery 1 and he reports he feels fine.

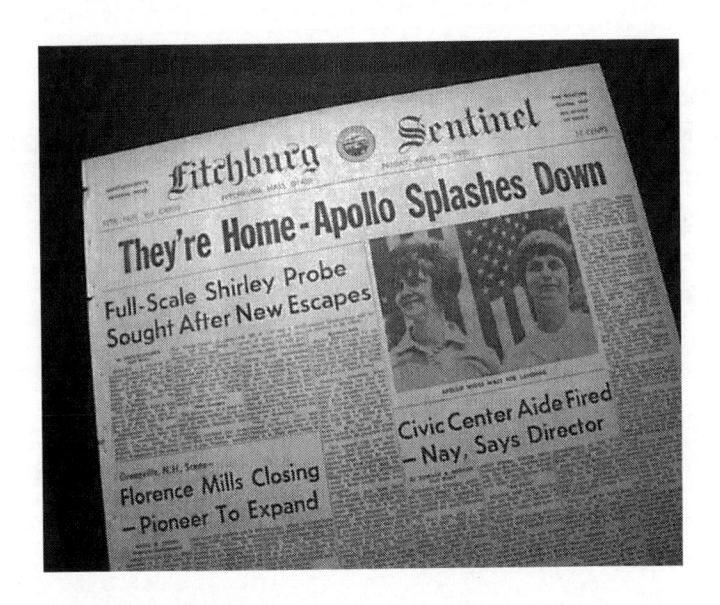

Walter Cronkite @WCronkiteCBSNews
The recovery helicopter is now flying back to land on the deck of the carrier Iwo Jima carrying its oh-so-precious cargo.

Walter Cronkite @WCronkiteCBSNews
Three men who 3 or 4 days ago,… well the odds weren't too high that they'd be making this short helicopter flight today.

Walter Cronkite @WCronkiteCBSNews
We are hearing that Mary Haise, wife of Fred Haise, is jubilant and thankful, as might be expected.

Walter Cronkite @WCronkiteCBSNews
Mrs. Haise spoke with President Nixon just moments ago and told him, "This is the most beautiful sight I have ever seen!"

Walter Cronkite @WCronkiteCBSNews
When the crew step of the helicopter and onto the deck of the recovery ship, that is when the cheers will ring out at Mission Control, Houston.

Walter Cronkite @WCronkiteCBSNews
That is also the moment when they break out the large cigars at Mission Control in Houston—a tradition established during the first Mercury flights.

Walter Cronkite @WCronkiteCBSNews
The crew of Apollo 13 have made it, thanks to the thousands of people on the ground in Houston and the prayers of millions around the world.

Walter Cronkite @WCronkiteCBSNews
And now the astronauts are on the deck of the Iwo Jima being cheered by a rapturous crew of thousands of the ship's sailors.

David Brinkley @DBNBCNews
The navy band onboard the USS Iwo Jima is now playing a march version of the tune Aquarius in fitting tribute to the tiny spacecraft that saved the lives of these three astronauts against all the odds.

Walter Cronkite @WCronkiteCBSNews
We understand the President has declared a national day of thanksgiving for Sunday and has telephoned Dr. Payne, the head of NASA, to congratulate him.

Walter Cronkite @WCronkiteCBSNews
And so the epic journey of Apollo 13 to the Moon, around the Moon and back to Earth with no help from the service propulsion system which was blown out by that explosion on Monday night, finally comes to a conclusion.

Walter Cronkite @WCronkiteCBSNews
A mission that will go down in history, perhaps, as a 'successful failure'. A mission that looked certain to be heading to end in tragedy ends instead in a spectacular recovery marveled at by much of the world.

The End

Thank you so much for reading. If you enjoyed reading, please consider posting a review on the book's page at Amazon. To see other Hashtag History books and to find out about upcoming publications, please visit our website at: http://www.hashtaghistories.com/

Major Sources

NASA documents and related sources

http://history.nasa.gov/SP-4029/Apollo_13h_Timeline.htm
http://www.timetoast.com/timelines/the-apollo-13-mission
http://www.hq.nasa.gov/office/pao/History/Timeline/apollo13chron.html
http://apollo13.spacelog.org/original/8/
http://www.hq.nasa.gov/pao/History/SP-350/ch-13-1.html

Apollo 13: Flight director loops

http://www.youtube.com/watch?v=KWfnY9cRXO4
http://www.youtube.com/watch?v=cnGaFXkzHZU
http://www.youtube.com/watch?v=o5wHChbahlI
http://www.youtube.com/watch?v=sTPNXGGTelM

Recorded live broadcasts from CBS, NBC and ABC news networks

http://www.youtube.com/watch?v=JKzcpMkwLXU

http://www.youtube.com/watch?v=58vFEOHSc1I
http://www.youtube.com/watch?v=i8BsEmyswaY
http://www.youtube.com/watch?v=hQZbRgc_mcQ
http://www.youtube.com/watch?v=2hBLoQAk72M
http://www.youtube.com/watch?v=b0QNX8q82PA
http://www.youtube.com/watch?v=SXTINUtVYz4
http://www.youtube.com/watch?v=KnZ7xGlZPHg
http://www.youtube.com/watch?v=Pop7CJzm7iE
http://www.youtube.com/watch?v=BJewO3gS88A
http://www.youtube.com/watch?v=6ir6GkUSyGQ
http://www.youtube.com/watch?v=5bKxssFKwHg
http://www.youtube.com/watch?v=I8jToufqrC8
http://www.youtube.com/watch?v=-xq1lkYOqEc
http://www.youtube.com/watch?v=SCxyO5PTRSs
http://www.youtube.com/watch?v=cmfMXKad_oI
http://www.youtube.com/watch?v=swTUBotqTRk
http://www.youtube.com/watch?v=xfUEgHS9rgg
http://www.youtube.com/watch?v=xfUEgHS9rgg
http://www.youtube.com/watch?v=gtX2hBBmHQw
http://www.youtube.com/watch?v=B-w1Fm6SSfU
http://www.youtube.com/watch?v=RU-N3oeETH4
http://www.youtube.com/watch?v=vqNIA_mMS0M
http://www.youtube.com/watch?v=3uIThShp6w4
http://www.youtube.com/watch?v=oKcT6bglDEM

Recommended Reading

Lost Moon: The Perilous Journey of Apollo 13. Jeffrey Kluger, James Lovell. ISBN: 978-0395670293

Apollo EECOM: Journey of a Lifetime. Sy Liebergot, David Harland. ISBN: 978-1894959889

Failure is not an Option: Gene Kranz. ISBN: 0743200799